SERGEI O. PROKOFIEFF, born in Moscow in 1954, studied fine arts and painting at the Moscow School of Art. He encountered anthroposophy in his youth, and soon made the decision to devote his life to it. He has been active as an author and lecturer since 1982, and in 1991 he co-founded the Anthroposophical Society in Russia. In Easter 2001 he became a member of the Executive Council of the General Anthroposophical Society in Dornach. He is the author of dozens of books, including *May Human Beings Hear It!*, *The Occult Significance of Forgiveness* and *The Appearance of Christ in the Etheric*.

PETER SELG, born in 1963 in Stuttgart, studied medicine in Witten-Herdecke, Zurich and Berlin. Until 2000, he worked as the head physician of the juvenile psychiatry department of Herdecke hospital in Germany. Dr Selg is now director of the Ita Wegman Institute for Basic Research into Anthroosophy (Arlesheim, Switzerland) and professor of medicine at the Alanus University of Arts and Social Sciences (Germany). He lectures extensively and is the author of numerous books, including *The Figure of Christ*, *The Agriculture Course* and *Rudolf Steiner and Christian Rosenkreutz*. He is married with five children.

Crisis in the Anthroposophical Society
and Pathways to the Future

Sergei O. Prokofieff · Peter Selg

TEMPLE LODGE

Translated from German by Willoughby Ann Walshe

Temple Lodge Publishing
Hillside House, The Square
Forest Row, RH18 5ES

www.templelodge.com

Published by Temple Lodge 2013

Originally published in German in two booklets under the titles *Die Identität der Allgemeinen Anthroposophischen Gesellschaft* (Peter Selg) and *Wie stehen wir heute vor Rudolf Steiner?* (Sergei O. Prokofieff) by Verlag des Ita Wegman Instituts, 2012

© Verlag des Ita Wegman Instituts 2012

This translation © Temple Lodge Publishing 2013

The moral rights of the authors have been asserted under the Copyright, Designs and Patents Act, 1988

All rights reserved. No part of this publication may be reproduced, stored in a retrieval system, or transmitted, in any form or by any means, electronic, mechanical, photocopying or otherwise, without the prior permission of the publishers

A catalogue record for this book is available from the British Library

ISBN 978 1 906999 43 8

Cover by Morgan Creative
Typeset by DP Photosetting, Neath, West Glamorgan
Printed and bound by Berforts, Herts.

Contents

Part I: Peter Selg

THE IDENTITY OF THE GENERAL ANTHROPOSOPHICAL SOCIETY

Preface	3
The New Beginning of the Anthroposophical Society in 1923/24 *Lecture: Basel, 14 March 2012*	9
The Challenges of the Present and Future *Lecture: Dornach, 30 March 2012*	37
Appendix: The Relation to the School of Spiritual Science. Teachers, Doctors and Priests in 1924	53

Part II: Sergei O. Prokofieff

HOW DO WE STAND BEFORE RUDOLF STEINER TODAY?

Preface	63
On the Anniversary of Rudolf Steiner's Death *Lecture: Dornach, 30 March 2012*	69
Afterword	91
Appendix: A Reflection on Peter Selg's Publication: *The Identity of the General Anthroposophical Society*	99
Notes	105
Bibliography	127

Part I

Peter Selg

THE IDENTITY OF THE GENERAL ANTHROPOSOPHICAL SOCIETY

Preface

The centennial of the founding of the Anthroposophical Society in December 1912 in Cologne, and even more so the condition of the world—and anthroposophy's situation in it—provide occasion and opportunity to think anew about the nature, tasks, and goals of the General Anthroposophical Society. The ageing of this Society and the criticism regarding its traditional methods of operation, which many young people decidedly interested in anthroposophy and Rudolf Steiner express, and which cause them to distance themselves from further approaching the Society and the School of Spiritual Science; the dubious situation in many anthroposophical institutions (or those originally proceeding from anthroposophy), whose spiritual substance, originality, and initiative-impetus are disappearing; and finally, the continual crises of the Dornach Goetheanum, which in the eyes of many members is experiencing a tragic development: These predicaments make it necessary to reflect upon the form which Rudolf Steiner once intended with the General Anthroposophical Society.

Substantive discussions about what *relevance* his original thoughts, conceptions, and initiatives have for our situation in the present and into the future, presume a real knowledge of this beginning—a knowledge that in many places no longer exists. The General Anthroposophical Society had and has a spiritual identity, a spiritual 'image' with concrete 'Leading Thoughts,' but it is apparent that among many members and administrators these contents are inadequately or all too vaguely known. They can presume that the essential purpose of the General Anthroposophical Society connected with Rudolf Steiner is of an historical nature and has no contemporary significance; it belongs to the twenties of the last century, and its accurate recognition and penetration is neither important nor useful in the context of historical documentation.

Actually, it is apparently not difficult to forget the spiritual identity of the General Anthroposophical Society, to suppress it from consciousness and skip over it; this makes room for one's own impulses and frees a person from the necessity of occupying himself with and confronting what is concrete, which Rudolf Steiner specifically intended—and towards which, with his waning life-forces, he applied himself until the end. Taking account of the more than eight decades since Rudolf

Steiner's death, the changing times, and, with this change, the corresponding necessity to make new decisions based on present-day circumstances—this approach appeals to many people and belongs to the self-consciousness of contemporary intellectuality. However, the problem with such an approach is obvious. Rudolf Steiner founded the General Anthroposophical Society neither arbitrarily nor accidentally, but as a future instrument for anthroposophy itself, whose nature he knew better than anyone else. What social *form* anthroposophical spiritual science needs in order, within the world, to endure its future challenges and crises, indeed to contribute something essential to the world's development, was his guiding question—and who, standing firmly on anthroposophical ground, had more to say than he? Rudolf Steiner lived in anthroposophy—and he lived, as no other anthroposophist since, in the world of becoming, so that the social, political, and spiritual forces, and the tensions and afflictions that configured the 20th century and the time following, determined anthroposophy further in an essential way.

If we look carefully at what Rudolf Steiner described as the tasks and problems of the Anthroposophical Society, and with which he was confronted, until his death, in trying to overcome gravely undesirable developments and conflicts, then the validity of his statements will have a lasting effect. What Rudolf Steiner spoke about and criticized in 1923 in many discussions still applies to the core areas of our Societal problems in 2012, even though these issues are seldom observed and overcome. Upon closer examination, Rudolf Steiner's statements prove prophetic and contemporary—which is really not surprising when one thinks of who Rudolf Steiner was and what a comprehensive viewpoint he possessed.

One can, however, ask what has actually happened with regard to these difficulties over the three-quarters of a century since his death, and about their possible progress and solution within the Anthroposophical Society—especially what forces of temptation, stubbornness and hindrance have worked further, and even today remain at least partially active. Why is it so difficult actually to understand and implement the 'intentions of the Christmas Conference' (in Rudolf Steiner's words), which represent a very concrete answer to the Anthroposophical Society's 'identity crisis', and which were conceptualized and formulated out of specific prerequisites and conditions for the activity of anthroposophy? In my view, it is obvious that the apparent misunderstanding and real ignorance is a conscious obstruction; here at work are not only unfortunate constellations of conditions and people, as well as personal tragedy, but also a calculated will—which, when viewed in its true perspective, intends to weaken and delay the fundamental impulse for civilization, demobilize and destroy its esoteric core, and let it fall into oblivion, along with the person and individuality—the being—Rudolf Steiner.

In the future, these correlations will be strongly reflected upon—and together with this, the questioning of one's own actions and responsibility with regard to the future of the General Anthroposophical Society. This responsibility in no way lies exclusively or even mainly in the hands of delegates or members of leading committees—so-called 'responsibility carriers'—but rests with every person for whom Rudolf Steiner's work and the spiritual–humanitarian impulse connected with him are an existential concern; this responsibility must also be perceived when the analysis of one's own being and ability turns out to be negative or depressing. Rudolf Steiner spoke about the 'good' and 'healthy feeling' of 'not being equal to a thing'[1]; that is, the continual awareness of everything lacking in oneself, in order to work productively with other people on the real continued development of the Anthroposophical Society, the Goetheanum, and anthroposophy in the world. He called this feeling 'good' and 'healthy', because it can immunize against the temptations of arrogance, vanity, and rhetoric, as well as pave and make possible a productive, modest path. That many people will tread this path in the future, raise themselves out of their supposed powerlessness, express themselves, and cooperate in helping the General Anthroposophical Society become a reality in the sense intended by Rudolf Steiner, is one of the hopes of the Goetheanum and the School of Spiritual Science. '*In order [. . .] to want to cooperate for the salvation of mankind, one must not be pessimistic, but believe in one's work. One must have courage really to think that one is in a position to realize what one considers to be right.*'[2] If this effort fails, then the Society prepared by Rudolf Steiner will without doubt die, gradually or abruptly, in the coming years and decades; and the Goetheanum as such, despite its exceedingly important Section-work and social relationships, will become spiritually and substantively insignificant. With this, however, something essential would be lost for many centuries.

★

In preparation for publication, two lectures that I held recently in Basel and at the Goetheanum about the General Anthroposophical Society's history and tasks, i.e., about its spiritual identity, have been slightly expanded. They were occasioned by the foundation of the Society in

Cologne—to be sure, not in the strict sense connected with a centennial celebration, but with respect to the being and creation of the social relationships that were founded—or more to the point *continued*—in 1912. 'Our work will advance in the same spirit, because we are concerned not with a substantive change, but only with a change of name that has become necessary for us', Rudolf Steiner said at the beginning of 1913, after the Anthroposophical Society was disentangled from the Theosophical Society.[3] The Society stood at the 'beginning of an important effort to strengthen and expand the *old* work'.[4] Actually, according to Rudolf Steiner's understanding, the Anthroposophical Society was not really founded, but emerged through Steiner's lectures and books, i.e., through the social community developing around their contents: 'Through those personalities who in this way learned what I had to say about the spiritual world, and through those who found the path to this method due to activity with some "theosophical direction", there formed within the framework of the Theosophical Society what later became the Anthroposophical Society.'[5] Understood in this way, the 'Anthroposophical Society' (or community) already existed spiritually-socially within the German Section of the Theosophical Society *before* 1912 'in a sort of embryonic life', as Rudolf Steiner emphasized,[6] and at this point had a clearly defined task: 'It originally had the task of confronting what was present in the Theosophical Society—and that was the traditional reception of age-old oriental wisdom—with the spirituality of occidental civilization containing the Mystery of Golgotha as its central point.'[7] In no way, however, do these words minimize what happened in December 1912 in Cologne,[8] which led to a further improvement and intensification at Christmastime 1923/24 in Dornach. The Cologne friends of the Anthroposophical Society are to be thanked heartily, because for Michaelmas this year they have organized an important conference in their city, to which an international audience has been invited and which can lead to an initiative for renewed consciousness of the General Anthroposophical Society's true tasks.

The following accounts are sketches. They are related (along with my study, *Rudolf Steiner's Intentions for the Anthroposophical Society*, published last year) to comments in the book *Rudolf Steiner, 1861–1925, Lebens- und Werkgeschichte* [*A History of his Life and Work*], to be published in November 2012, where they are further explained and supplemented. I have some friends to thank for their emphatic request to print an edition of both lectures. Originally I did not intend to publish them, because, as is known, much has already appeared about these issues without anything having changed substantially as a result. Whether further books on this subject are necessary or helpful, and who—and in what position and situation—will read them at all can definitely be critically scrutinized. However, giving up such hope for the future is surely not what Rudolf Steiner wanted. 'The person who loves sees the future everywhere. Therefore, there is a close connection between love and hope' (Michael Bauer[9]).

Ita Wegman Institute, Arlesheim *Peter Selg*
Easter 2012

Programm der Delegiertentagung vom 25.- 28.Februar 1923.

Sonntag morgen 11 Uhr Vorführung von Eurythmie der Schülerinnen von Frau Fels und Fräulein Köhler.
  nachmittags menschliche Fühlungnahme mit den Delegierten.
  abends im Sieglehaus (nicht Landhausstrasse) Begrüssung 8 Uhr durch Herrn Leinhas, Dr. Kolisko Bericht über die Lage, Aussprache der Delegierten - daraus Entwicklung des Programms für den weiteren Verlauf.

Montag morgen 10-12½ Uhr Dreigliederung, Dr. Unger, evtl. mit darauf folgender Diskussion, danach, falls noch Zeit vorhanden, Komtag - Herrn Leinhas, Waldorfschule - Fräul.Dr.v.Heydebrand
  nachmittags 3 - 6 Uhr das, was am vormittag nicht mehr zu verhandeln möglich war (evgl. die beiden Themata des Vormittags Komtag und Waldorfschule, Forschungsinstitut, Klinisch-therapeutisches Institut, Strakosch, Dr. Palmer.
  abends 8 Uhr religiöse Bewegung - Dr. Hahn, Rittelmeyer, Unger, Uehli, Bock - : Dr. Palmer.

Dienstag früh 10 - 12½ Uhr Wissenschaft und Anthroposophie - Ueberbrückung der Kluft zwischen beiden, Dr. Kolisko,- Hochschulbund : Dr. Stein und Maikowsky.
  nachmittags 2½ - 4½ Uhr Gegnerschaft : Dr. Stein, Rittelmeyer etc., Information über die Gegner, Ziel, Gegenfeldzug.
  nachmittags 5 Uhr : Eurythmie in der Landhausstrasse
  8 Uhr : Vortrag Dr. Steiner (evtl. muss der Abend zur weiteren Diskussion verwandt werden und der Vortrag Dr. Steiner's muss auf einen anderen Tag verlegt werden.

Mittwoch vormittag 10 - 12½ Uhr : Innere Arbeit, Früchte der Arbeit, Anerkennung dieser Früchte, Zyklen, Studienkreise, Einführungskurse, Organisation, Vertretung nach aussen.
  nachmittags 2½ - 4½ Uhr : Bund für freies Geistesleben, Zeitung und Verlag
  nachmittags 5 Uhr Eurythmie in der Landhausstrasse
  abends 8 Uhr : Vortrag Dr. Steiner.

Handwritten notes by Rudolf Steiner
From GA 259, p. 360

1. The New Beginning of the Anthroposophical Society in 1923/24

Lecture: Basel, 14 March 2012

'And that is what I ask our friends for again and again, as a priority; for we now face the urgent need to make the Society an active, effective entity in the world. That, my dear friends, is what we need. It would of course be very desirable for the centre at Dornach not to collapse, but for friends to be found who can help ...'

Rudolf Steiner, November 1922[10]

Dear friends,

Never had Rudolf Steiner spoken more clearly about the task and form of the Anthroposophical Society than in the days, weeks and months following the burning of the first Goetheanum. The Society itself, he said at that time, contained 'something ruinous'[11] and it was necessary to develop an understanding with 'sincere love'[12] for what is inadequate and insufficient within the Anthroposophical Society, with a will for relentless honesty and clarity—*'so that such things will not just be talked about, but through insight into the mistakes, through sharp judgement of the errors, it will be recognized what must be done in the future'*.[13] Rudolf Steiner wanted 'conscious research' and 'consciousness of responsibility' at least from the leading members of the Society; he favoured neither internal assignments of blame nor complaints about the external opposition, which he presumed to be known. A few days after the fire, he added further: 'As long as we are our own worst internal enemies, and so long as we indeed demand of ourselves to work upon an occult basis, we should not be surprised when a terrible opposition attacks from the outside' (6 January 1923[14]). After the burning of the Goetheanum, which he viewed as a symptom, Rudolf Steiner left no doubt that the Anthroposophical Society's existence was at risk—*'thus, it cannot exist as it was before'* (22 January 1923[15]). He applied all his energy to the necessary methods of working for consciousness and reorganization, and from the beginning of September 1923 travelled twice a week to Stuttgart for night-long meetings and discussions—because this Society, this organization, was so important to him! Due to massive external opposition, he reduced the public lectures on anthroposophy noticeably. As Christoph Lindenberg documented, Rudolf Steiner held only eleven public lectures about anthroposophy in 1923, less than one per month—in 1922 there were 79, more than one per week.

Rudolf Steiner's focus on Society problems, which was a determining factor for the year 1923 in the Anthroposophical Society's history, was in no way new in terms of content—though he had never before unfolded these considerations with such intensity and temporal concentration. In the preceding years, in the most various places and in different connections, he continually made critical remarks about the Society's situation as well as about the behaviour of members and those in positions of leadership—substantive remarks, as distinct from aphoristic statements. At the beginning of December 1922, in the course of an internationally attended pedagogical course, he summarized:

> You see, during the past years we have had, at least in Central Europe, a very strong expansion of the Anthroposophical Movement. Today the Anthroposophical Movement is a factor in the Central European world. It is a factor as spiritual movement. We have [however] no organization to direct and guide this movement. The Anthroposophical Society—this must be said, for it is good when it is known—the Anthroposophical Society is not in a position to carry the Anthroposophical Movement. For the Anthroposophical Society is so strongly permeated with sectarian inclinations that it just cannot support the Anthroposophical Movement as it is today, as it has become.[16]

As Rudolf Steiner continually depicted it, the Anthroposophical Society hadn't matured and wasn't appropriate for anthroposophy—for its spiritual content, which had advanced further, and for its concrete active impulses, which had precipitated into numerous newly founded organizations. The Society—as Society—lagged behind all of this. In 1923, after the fire, Rudolf Steiner spoke about its urgent need for '*inner consolidation and positive work*'.[17] Regarding this 'positive work', Rudolf Steiner included the perception of concrete tasks of significance for civilization. It is well-known that from the beginning on—i.e., since 1902—the Anthroposophical Society had acquired a context of spiritual study: a form of spiritual community centred on the being Anthroposophy. This was Rudolf Steiner's intention; at the same time, however, he never left any doubt that tasks established for this Society could not and should never be exhausted. It was certainly not only a matter of people in the Anthroposophical Society being able to find new life-content, and through the Anthroposophical Society, a new social organization with new relationships and encounters. All this was important, even essential and indispensable, yet still of only a preparatory nature. As early as 1905 Rudolf Steiner wrote in a statement: 'To work through the ideas of spiritual science means increasing the capability for social activity. In this regard it is not so important what thoughts a person receives through spiritual science, but what a person *makes out of his thoughts*'.[18] The Anthroposophical Society doesn't want to educate people who are 'isolated and unusual', 'rather, it wants to produce people who indeed are *effective and active in the world*'.[19] An anthroposophist 'in the real sense of the word' is a person who is deeply in touch with the 'nerve of the times'[20]— undoubtedly Rudolf Steiner assumed from the beginning that study groups forming would one day become practicing communities. The original Christians had internalized Christian learning, preached and healed sick people; i.e., they took initiative in their time and with regard to the needs of their time—and the later Rosicrucian community appeared as a practicing therapeutic group from the beginning as well. In 1907, regarding anthroposophy and its Society or community, Rudolf Steiner said:

> People who unite in the movement, which we call the movement for theosophically oriented spiritual science, should feel themselves to be like the core from which the energy for a new social form emanates. [...] What can come to social formation from other directions can be very useful. But it must be worked upon: True social renewal can only come from spiritual impulses.[21]

Rudolf Steiner always made clear that recognition of anthroposophical spiritual science in public life and civilization as a whole could only be achieved through productive and innovative work in various areas of life, i.e., in perceiving tasks arising from general, universal social interests: 'Only when everywhere in theosophical circles there arises a thorough comprehension: that everything depends on what we learn being made to the greatest possible extent fruitful for all conditions of life, not merely theorized about—only then will life open to spiritual science with understanding. Otherwise, people will continue to consider theosophy as a type of religious sect of individual, peculiar dreamers. However, when they accomplish positive, useful spiritual work, then an understanding approval of the spiritual-scientific movement will not fail to come about in the long run.'[22]

There is no doubt that in response to these statements and intentions over one-and-a-half decades, Rudolf Steiner met with very little understanding among *those* very people who regularly came to his lectures and read his books—and who were essentially occupied with their own personal development. As 'homeless souls', they sought help and perspectives for their personal path; Rudolf Steiner knew and respected this, without however abandoning the above-stated perspectives. He worked with immeasurable patience and positivity, which upon closer examination of his biography is revealed to a deeply moving extent—he worked with a broad scope and faith in the future, which seemed nearly unbreakable. The scientific, social and political problems and challenges that Rudolf Steiner observed at the turn to the 20th century were enormous; however, he gave a great part of his time and energy to developing a spiritual community, which made exceedingly slow progress and in which there were numerous obstacles. Rudolf Steiner worked with the people given him by destiny without complaining, and all the while looking towards the future.

★

This does not contradict the fact that his lectures during and after World War I highlighted ever more clearly and alarmingly what disaster and drama had befallen civilization—and that other active impulses would be necessary in the *immediate future*. Effective time and possibilities for the Anthroposophical Society were surely running out; nevertheless, the first initiatives started to unfold from among the membership after 1918 (17 years after the beginning of Rudolf Steiner's spiritual-scientific activity in the narrow sense). With the Movement for the Threefold Social Structure—out of which proceeded at least the first Free Waldorf School, the 'Der Kommende Tag' association and indirectly, also the Clinical-Therapeutic Institute (as well as the natural-scientific research institution) in Stuttgart—there occurred after 1919 the first turnaround and renewal. The Anthroposophical Society as such, however, remained largely unaffected by this, even in Stuttgart. It continued with the branch work—as Rudolf Steiner intended—but also occupied itself with internal problems and social tensions, which tended to be centred among personalities. Even though Rudolf Steiner had alluded to this problem for years, it was never overcome, at least not in circles of leading administrators and lecturers, despite all his books and lectures regarding soul-spiritual training. '*They sit in their chairs, act like they are directors, and people don't want to have anything to do with them*', wrote Rudolf Steiner in 1923 of the council members of the German Anthroposophical Society,[23] who by and large had lost their relation to the 'base' of anthroposophists, as well as to social reality. An Anthroposophical Society represented and administered in this self-centred way not only gave little support to anthroposophy, but also damaged its image, as Rudolf Steiner emphasized. Anthroposophical spiritual science, 'through the detour of the Anthroposophical Society', was being totally misunderstood by the world,[24] and was becoming a 'hindrance' for the Anthroposophical Movement[25]—its real spirituality and practical life, to which, as of 1919, such an outstandingly active institution as the Free Waldorf School belonged. Rudolf Steiner expected a real interest in and relationship to the world on the part of members and leading representatives of the Anthroposophical Society; ever and again he said that it is a matter of making the problems and needs of present-day civilization one's own and, with the help of anthroposophy, working productively on them instead of isolating oneself self-centredly, convinced of possessing higher truths: 'The misery that can be seen today within civilization should be a summons to enter into a supersensible consideration of humanity and the world. We can only do this when we are aware of what is going on in the world.'[26] 'What good is it to continually tell people we are not a sect, when we act like we are a sect ... ?'[27]

Dismayed, Rudolf Steiner witnessed in the years before the burning of the Goetheanum how arrogantly the Anthroposophical Society as a whole had treated young people, who, due to their existential war-experiences, welcomed the Threefold Social Structure and were interested in anthroposophy and its Society. Many, even the majority of these young people, were more than astonished—some even shocked—by the Anthroposophical Society, its habits, activities and social forms, as they had personally reported to Rudolf Steiner. 'They were really seeking [anthroposophy], but didn't find it. At most they found: When you want to be a true anthroposophist you must believe in the etheric body and reincarnation and so forth.'[28] Rudolf Steiner well understood how alienated the young people felt with regard to the 'talking *about* spirit' instead of true spirit-filled speaking and acting; and how intensively they experienced the circulation in Society circles of 'thoughts imitated' from Rudolf Steiner's work: thoughts and ideas that had not become internalized into actual experience and seeds of development for the individuality. 'Thoughts that have no heart' did not interest this generation of youth, which had had enough of their academic and other teachers' pseudo-intellectuality, and witnessed that resistance against the nationalistic World War euphoria had neither proceeded from German universities and intellectual institutions, nor was an attempt made at fundamental social reform following the War. The circle of young people that had formed around Rudolf Steiner's work, however, didn't find the new beginning they sought within the Society. Members of the Anthroposophical Society often spoke about the human 'individuality' or 'I'—but without experiencing the consequences of these thoughts in social behaviour and without the power to meet people; lacking interest for other people. Conversely, Rudolf Steiner said: 'When a person goes through life and meets individual people he must have an open heart, an open mind for the person. With each individual encounter one must be in a position to develop a completely new feeling for the person. One only meets someone else correctly by seeing a new person in each individual. For this reason, every person who meets us has the right that we develop a new feeling for him. For when we come with a general concept and say how the person should be in a certain regard, then we do him wrong. With each definition of a person we actually put blinkers on that stop us seeing the individual.'[29] Referring to the Anthroposophical Society, he continued:

> The Anthroposophical Society needs reorganization. It should be possible that in it human individualities can—according to their own unique nature and the possibilities open to them—enjoy life, really be active and find an atmosphere in which, continuing their education, they can breathe.[30]

However, this did not happen in 1923—just as in previous years. Therefore, many younger people remained outside the Anthroposophical Society, even though many of them applied for membership cards—having confidence in Rudolf Steiner and wanting to hear his internal lectures. Depressed and frustrated, they engaged themselves only conditionally in the organizational forms and association-structures of the Anthroposophical Society, and instead participated in the destiny of the Free Waldorf School, the Threefold Social Structure and other initiatives—in proceedings which the Anthroposophical Society did not consider to be its own tasks, even though Rudolf Steiner already pointed out in 1920 'that thereby [with the founding of these institutions] something has happened that affects us all to such an extent that we must concern ourselves *with our comportment*'.[31] During summer 1920 in Stuttgart he pointed out:

> We have organizations that must not fail, that must succeed—for which there should be no discussion that they could fail in any way, and of which we must say today: They will succeed. Yet, so that they do not devour the original Anthroposophical Movement, it is necessary that *everyone* really cooperate on what should result morally from our decades-long work, really become engaged. It is certainly necessary that *everyone* cooperate.[32]

Nevertheless, the Waldorf School and the other institutions thereafter remained 'foreign bodies' in the life of the Anthroposophical Society. They fought for their existence in the midst of difficult economic conditions and were exposed to some massive public criticism—however, they received little to no substantial support from the Anthroposophical Society. At the Stuttgart delegation gathering in February 1923, Rudolf Steiner personally read a position statement by senior Waldorf School students, who spoke about their imminent departure from the school and the necessity for an anthroposophical high-school facility, for whose construction they longingly hoped. '*Why is the eventual guidance of an Anthroposophical Society one of the most important questions?*' Rudolf Steiner asked after reading the students' petition.[33] The senior students' inquiry and Rudolf Steiner's question, however, met with the same response as had many other such initiatives, including a repeated appeal to create a 'World School Association' so as to finance and maintain facilities for free spiritual life. Instead of affirming these, there took place in Stuttgart and at other Society meetings countless speeches and personal opinions, subjective concerns, vague motions and a general tangled confusion. All of this led nowhere—and the Anthroposophical Society was far removed from perceiving the tasks '*for which people outside can also have respect*'.[34] According to Rudolf Steiner, as an esoteric community having a mission with exoteric action to perform, it should become an effective factor of modern civilization, something 'that has something to say at present'[35]; it should take a position, represent an 'active content' and stand for something. Proceeding from an image of the human being other than that of contemporary materialism, Rudolf Steiner expected strong initiative from the Anthroposophical Society and its leadership—as well as the courage to represent uncommon positions publicly. The Anthroposophical Society was not in the right position or lacked the will for this, and apparently very few of its members understood what Rudolf Steiner meant and expected of them. '*That is essentially what I always wanted to ask and now request of our friends, because today we are faced with the urgent necessity of making the Society an active, effective entity in the world. This is what we need, my dear friends.*'[36]

Not once did leading anthroposophists or work centres view as their own tasks the conflict with the aggressive opponents of anthroposophy that were appearing—rather, they left these tasks to individual fighters like Eugen Kolisko, Walter Johannes Stein or Louis Werbeck, although Rudolf Steiner spoke repeatedly about the explosive force of the different attacks and the response necessary on the part of the Anthroposophical Society ('*if* [...] *in response to the opposition nothing is done, then the mission of anthroposophy will fail*'[37]). When it was requested that a presentation responding to the opponents of anthroposophy be removed from the programme of the February 1923 Stuttgart delegation-gathering in order to make room for more positive content, Rudolf Steiner deliberated his complete withdrawal from the Anthroposophical Society. However, he decided to remain and continue his efforts in this regard. Nevertheless, he made it clear that a decisive conflict with the aggressive critics of the Anthroposophical Society would be necessary in the future—and to be sure, on the part of the Anthroposophical Society and its directors as such. He expressed himself vehemently about the just-as-naïve and dangerous efforts of individual anthroposophists wanting to enter into 'dialogue' with opponents like Max Dessoir and behave in a conciliatory fashion to all objections and opinions. Instead of treading this wrong path, Rudolf Steiner implored members and leading committees of the Anthroposophical Society to finally realize what forces were at work here to destroy truth in a calculated manner. According to Rudolf Steiner it is not a matter of entering into a contentious 'discourse', but to work out what *methods* of falsification, lies and aggressive defamation were being employed, and also what psychopathological issues many of the critics exhibit. 'We must become accustomed to bringing things to a completely different level.'[38]

★

Rudolf Steiner saw not only massive problems within the Anthroposophical Society and its guiding committees, but also within the anthroposophical institutions themselves, which after their establishment increasingly lost contact with the Society. All teachers of the Stuttgart Waldorf School remained anthroposophists; but they increasingly invested their energies in maintaining and developing their school, and kept themselves removed from matters of the Anthroposophical Society, its meetings, work-groups and problems. These meetings were time-intensive and only minimally progressive in content; in some cases they were old-fashioned and determined or thwarted by personal aspirations. Instead of cooperating further, the teachers focused attention on the school. Rudolf Steiner understood their behaviour, but left no doubt that this would have negative consequences in the future—for the (at least medium-term-endangered) spirituality of the school *and* for the Anthroposophical Society, which without decisive assistance from personalities taking initiative would continue to stagnate and become isolated from life: 'There should not be a separate Waldorf School movement, a movement for free spiritual life, a movement for religious renewal; rather, all of this can thrive only when it is seen as part of the parent movement, the Anthroposophical Movement.'[39] 'One can [...] be an excellent Waldorf School teacher and a poor anthroposophist, one can be an outstanding worker in any other organization and a poor anthroposophist. This is just how it is: All the individual organizations have grown out of the topsoil of anthroposophy and one should realize that one must above all remain a real anthroposophist, that one may not deny this centre, not as Waldorf School teacher, Kommende Tag employee, researcher, doctor—that one must never even remotely have the conviction to say: I have no time for general anthroposophical affairs. *Otherwise, there surely could be life for some time in each of these institutions, because anthroposophy as such contains and imparts real life, but it cannot maintain this life permanently. It would dry up, even for individual institutions.*'[40] It was clear that Rudolf Steiner spoke not only about what was imminent, but also about developments in the distant future, which he undoubtedly saw coming. Rudolf Steiner complained in 1923 that general anthroposophical publications were hardly read any more in the Waldorf School by teachers, and that there was little interest in the crisis-riddled development of the Society. When Waldorf School teacher Erich Schwebach—who was highly regarded by Rudolf Steiner—expressed in a crisis-meeting of the Society negative and pessimistic thoughts about the intention of the entire Society discussion, Rudolf Steiner said to him in a direct and exceptionally sharp tone:

> I know that sitting here are personalities who consider it entirely unnecessary to occupy themselves with the question of consolidating the Anthroposophical Society. If one had never dealt with these things, if one had never made an effort, then you [Mr Schwebach] would not be here today! Then there would have been no funds from which the Waldorf School could be fed. You can be sure it was different once. Because the Society was founded out of life, the possibility was created that you sit here today—and can find that everything is unfruitful. If it had always been so—if, for example, many people at the beginning-point of the Society had acted in the manner that you are now acting, then it wouldn't be possible for you to sit here today. You are like the famous person who wants to pull himself up by the tufts of his own hair. Therefore, you are obliged to justify the matter more deeply. Why don't you say what is important, what you are lacking here and what could elevate the matter? Life is not there merely to be pleasant. If it is only a matter of pleasantries one cannot hold Circle of Thirty meetings. Why don't you do it better? One can also sit here and indeed not be present.[41]

Since autumn 1919 Rudolf Steiner knew about the Stuttgart Waldorf School teachers' workload and their time commitments. Nevertheless, he considered their increasing disinterest in matters of the Anthroposophical Society to be fatal. People working for the Anthroposophical Society in different areas of life must be concerned—he said repeatedly—that the 'streams' of anthroposophy continue to flow within the Society from which they all originated. The Waldorf teachers as well as members of the 'Kommende Tag', the Movement for the Threefold Social Structure, the clinical-therapeutic institute or the research faculty give back to the Anthroposophical Society the strength it needs for its further existence. Rudolf Steiner always considered the Anthroposophical Society—despite all of its immense weaknesses and crises—still as the central organ of activity, the spiritual community for anthroposophy. The majority of young, initiative-bearing, highly talented people who were active in the Waldorf School and other institutions could and must support the Anthroposophical Society and help it to find its way out of its crisis and to become future-oriented ('Anthroposophy must not devolve into habit'[42]). He expected no turning away from this Society, but an increased attention to it.

★

Thereby, during the entire year of 1923, Rudolf Steiner made it clear that he thoroughly appreciated and considered extremely important the spiritual work that those in the Anthroposophical Society had accomplished over nearly two decades. Rudolf Steiner's extensive lecture courses about anthroposophy had taken place within the Society; the organ of the Society had made them possible, and many people had found a connection with the course-content through intensive spiritual-idealistic work and at least some meditative contemplation. In addition, the Anthroposophical Society had developed in its ranks a new connection to the dead, to members who had left the earthly life—as well as to other individualities, whom Rudolf Steiner considered important and continually spoke highly of.[43] However, in 1923, he also made clear that the real esoteric, internal realm of the Anthroposophical Society had experienced a distinct weakening; important personalities had died early, and in their stead, others in the Society had created the scope and influence to follow their own goals and purposes—and misused the Society-connections consciously or unconsciously for their personal intentions. They spoke 'for' the Anthroposophical Society and assumed the status of a 'representative' without being truly connected with the internal goals of the spiritual community around Rudolf Steiner. In 1919, many things of a compromising and diplomatic nature occurred in the Anthroposophical Society, in the context of large public conferences and increasing exoteric orientation. Rudolf Steiner had agreed upon and accompanied the step to make things public; however, he continued to work esoterically in the Society and encouraged members to bring their participation in contemporary world-destiny into connection with a deepened relation to the being of Anthroposophy. Instead of adapting to modern thought-, emotional- and behavioural-methods, Rudolf Steiner wanted 'courageous' work 'out of the innermost core'[44]—in the Waldorf School, the Movement for the Threefold Social Structure and in all other fields, as well as the Anthroposophical Society itself:

> The only proper course we can pursue is to tell the world what we have found through anthroposophy itself, and then wait and see how many people are able to understand it. We certainly cannot approach the world with the core material of anthroposophy in the hope that there might be a party or a person who can be won over. That is impossible. That is contrary to the fundamental circumstances governing the existence of the Anthroposophical Movement. Take a

women's movement or a social movement, for instance, where it is possible to take the view that we should join and compromise our position because its members' views may incline towards anthroposophy in one way or another; that is absolutely impossible. What matters is to have enough inner security regarding anthroposophy to be able to advocate it under any circumstances.[45]

According to Rudolf Steiner, every consideration of external things, 'be it recognition, be it success, be it opposition and hostility' leads to a 'damaging of the spiritual life that should be cultivated in such a movement'.[46] In contrast to this, Rudolf Steiner described what was necessary and required by the times: productive work out of the internal centre of anthroposophy—within the Anthroposophical Society as well as within those establishments that have arisen from it. He expressed criticism towards the previous work of the anthroposophical research institute—with the exception of Lilly Kolisko's activity—but also the Stuttgart Clinic from which he had expected a much different, more decisive start. Much that was put forward in the framework of 'scientific discourse' seemed to Rudolf Steiner exceptionally conventional and intellectually abstract, and hardly impressive in its results. Rudolf Steiner wanted *actual* research results and accomplishments from the various institutions of the Anthroposophical Movement—not only meetings, conferences and articles in their own publications, which touch on theoretical questions without being the expression of a really successful breakthrough. 'The opposition may be ever so great, but we must not allow our conduct to be such that they are proven correct. It is impossible to prevail against this opposition with the building of the Goetheanum, this School of Spiritual Science, when it can be proven that nothing scientific is accomplished.'[47] The professional courses, which Rudolf Steiner held for natural scientists and doctors after 1919, contained many significant research questions and themes; yet they were evaluated by their audiences as hardly productive—and very little of the scientific activity hoped for was achieved.

All of this did not belong to the core area of the General Anthroposophical Society. On the other hand, however, it was clear that it did concern the Society—and it should create the spiritual space out of which individual anthroposophists active in various areas could gain *and adhere* to their innermost work-impulse; i.e., in which each of them could meet the being of Anthroposophy again. Based on this, it was clearly understandable why Rudolf Steiner connected each further intensification in exoteric activity with a corresponding deepening in the esoteric area; and further, why he so highly esteemed the Anthroposophical Society despite, or especially because of, its tasks for civilization. If this was not accomplished by the General Anthroposophical Society, then the work initiated in the different areas would lead to a weakening of the anthroposophical intention, and at least in the mid-term, culminate in an 'identity crisis' and successively alienate anthroposophy's original contribution to civilization. If Waldorf School teachers failed to maintain and further develop their connection to the Anthroposophical Society's spiritual community—as the fundamental active body of anthroposophy—then their school would one day be degraded to a pedagogical reform project whose spiritual signature was indistinct, and would show signs of arbitrariness. The Anthroposophical Society was inseparably connected with the establishments that emerged from it and had to carry their destiny, in light and shadow—a fact with respect to which Rudolf Steiner iterated many details in 1923. The establishments had their effect on the Society and were also identified with Rudolf Steiner and anthroposophy.

*

In 1923 Rudolf Steiner reminded the Anthroposophical Society continually not only about its responsibilities—and thereby about its reason for being—but he also assisted or attempted, at least, to help it substantially. With his impressive descriptions about the history of the Anthroposophical Society and Movement, Rudolf Steiner began in the summer of 1923 to clarify the destiny of the people who had been led to the Anthroposophical Society.[48] These were undoubtedly lectures about self-knowledge, which Rudolf Steiner held in Dornach; they were intended to help young members to better understand the peculiarities of the 'homeless souls' of the older generation—as well as themselves. On the other hand, Rudolf Steiner spoke repeatedly in the course of 1923 about the younger generation's special destiny-circumstance; about the vitality of their appearance and their own will, against the background of their prenatal experiences. In 1924 Rudolf Steiner expanded both themes in an impressive and quite detailed manner; these motifs were also heard especially in 1923 in the context of his efforts to 'consolidate and bring a more positive direction' into the Society, and upon examination were an important contribution to spiritual community-building, deeper understanding and a possible cooperation among generations. Moreover, Rudolf Steiner held various lectures concerning the *solidarity* of anthroposophical spiritual-scientific work, in a subtle explanation of what spiritual work in the Society could or should occur across generations—between the people and in association with the esoteric core of anthroposophy. Various comments made by Rudolf Steiner in setting these goals revealed the possible spiritual-social substance of the Anthroposophical Society of the future, and thereby a central aspect of its inner identity. Rudolf Steiner spoke in the course of the Stuttgart delegate-gathering about an 'awakening' to the soul-spirit of anthroposophists among one another, an awakening in consummating the mutual spiritual study, of receiving the being of Anthroposophy internally within the Society; and he said, among other things: 'Now we want to receive such wonderful ideas from anthroposophy, from these proclamations by the spiritual world, we want to penetrate everything that can be said further about the ether body, astral body and so forth theoretically, but we still don't understand the spiritual world. We begin to develop the first understanding for the spiritual world when we awaken to the soul-spiritual nature of other people. Then the real understanding for anthroposophy begins. Yes, it is incumbent on us to proceed from the condition for a real understanding of anthroposophy, which can be called: the awakening of a person to the spiritual-soul nature of others. The force for this awakening can result when spiritual idealism is implanted into a human community.'[49] 'The Anthroposophical Society may appear this or that way in certain epochs—anthroposophy is independent of any Anthroposophical Society and can be found independently of it. It can certainly also be found in a special way, in that one learns to awaken to another person; and in this way, out of this awakening, community-building results. For one always awakens to something new in relation to the people with whom one is together; therefore, one remains together with them. There are inner spiritual reasons for this. This must be understood more and more within the Anthroposophical Society; and, essentially, all that is offered for the progress of the Anthroposophical Society must be penetrated by forces which in the end lead to anthroposophy as such.'[50] In various lectures from 1923—and for the first time in his entire work—Rudolf Steiner spoke about the meeting with the 'being' Anthroposophy as a 'person' within the Anthroposophical Society or community. According to him, members of the Anthroposophical Society are committed to this being; it is their own centre, their mutual goal and the foundation for their social connection:

Anthroposophy is actually an invisible person who walks among visible people, and towards whom we must show the greatest responsibility for as long as we are a small group. Anthroposophy is someone who must be understood as an invisible person, as someone with a real existence, who should be consulted in the individual actions of our lives.

Thus, if connections form among people—friendships, groups, and so on—at a time when the group of anthroposophists is still small, it is all the more necessary to consult and to be able to justify all one's actions before this invisible person.

This necessity will, of course, apply less and less as anthroposophy spreads. But as long as it remains the property of a small group of people, it is thoroughly necessary for every action to follow from consultation with the human being Anthroposophy. That Anthroposophy should be seen as a living being is an essential condition of its existence. [This condition] will be allowed to die only when its group of supporters has expanded immeasurably. What we require, then, is a real earnestness towards the invisible person I have just spoken about. This deep earnestness must, so to say, grow with every passing day. If this deep earnestness grows, then there can be no doubt that everything yet to been done will be inaugurated and carried further in the right way.[51]

Anthroposophists today must not think that they have merely the same responsibility which future anthroposophists will have when they exist by the million rather than the thousand. When limited numbers are active in the vanguard of a movement, they have to show responsibility of a much higher order. It means that they are obliged to show greater courage, greater energy, greater patience, greater tolerance and, above all, greater truthfulness in every respect. [...] Irrespective of the fact that individual anthroposophists exist, a feeling should have developed, and must develop among them that Anthroposophy exists as a separate being, who moves about among us, as it were, and towards whom we carry a responsibility in every moment of our lives.[52]

★

A further aid for positively consolidating and substantiating the Society— along with clarifying the current and spiritual-historical situation and commenting about the spiritual-social work in view of the 'being

Anthroposophia'—was, finally, Rudolf Steiner's preparation for an international or General Anthroposophical Society, to be formed on the basis of autonomous national Societies. In 1923, Rudolf Steiner encouraged the creation of such national Societies in all countries in which a sufficient number of anthroposophists lived and worked, as prerequisite for an intended international alliance. Undoubtedly, for him it was from the start a matter of overcoming the former centring of anthroposophy on Germany—in view of the political–economic conditions and the situation of the German national Society—and of laying the prerequisites for creating an international association, a collaboration that should also mean an 'affiliation' with Dornach as the future centre of the School of Spiritual Science in neutral Switzerland. Since the beginning of his activity in the German Section of the Theosophical Society in October 1902, Rudolf Steiner always had a primary concern for expanding modern spiritual science internationally, as well as creating a worldwide organization of people joined together spiritually. In 1923 he said about anthroposophy: 'When we want to grasp anthroposophy in the right sense in an historical connection, for the present historical moment, we must find an international means of communicating throughout the entire world, a means of communication through which people find one another, a means of dialogue which at the same time lies on a level higher than language.'[53] For many years—and also in the terrible period of World War I—Rudolf Steiner had spoken about this: that anthroposophy is in a position to form the basis of a new understanding of the human being, beyond the boundaries of ethnic origin—and the Goetheanum had from the beginning the task of providing the place for such union, the place for mutual consciousness-formation and international cooperation. 'That in the future a much stronger connection, the working of anthroposophists from all countries, must come about', Rudolf Steiner emphasized forcefully once more in 1923 in the course of establishing autonomous national Societies in various countries.[54] It is a matter of creating an 'understanding throughout the whole world'[55] and on the basis of the national Societies, establishing a 'unified structure' of a 'General Anthroposophical Society' as 'world Society'; a newly conceived Anthroposophical Society *that finally really works*'.[56] Rudolf Steiner didn't want a hierarchical communal organization administered from Dornach and he didn't want an international association to 'even out' the differences; he wanted rather the intensified cooperation, decision-making and improvement of regional- and working-groups. Therefore, he allowed the formation of autonomous national Societies to have absolute precedence over the intended alliance, and attached importance to each individual delegate, who had a valid 'statute' determined independently by his country, coming to Dornach at the end of the year to create the 'world Society'. This goal consisted of creating an organization that should work spiritually and socially worldwide, with the special conditions of the individual countries and at the same time within the consciousness of a larger, higher organization. 'There must [in an internationally effective Anthroposophical Society] be a really professional, objective spirit, which can be documented for the world.'[57] '*So that everyone who is in it knows: he represents a great matter in the world who is an anthroposophist . . .*'[58]

Crisis-meetings with leading members of the Anthroposophical Society—in which Rudolf Steiner so clearly articulated the orientation of exoteric and esoteric responsibility that he expected from the Anthroposophical Society in the future—took place primarily and almost solely in Stuttgart, which was not only the central location of anthroposophical initiatives but also, since 1921, the seat of the Anthroposophical Society's Executive Council. Statements made there by Rudolf Steiner applied in principle to all countries in which anthroposophists were active in community organizations. The principles of initiative and representation should in the future apply to all national Societies, and should be followed strictly. In the course of 1923 Rudolf Steiner spoke repeatedly about the necessity of a real 'news organ' informing anthroposophists in all countries about their international spiritual activities and initiatives—'individual anthroposophists should have an opportunity to form a picture of what is happening here or there in the world concerning anthroposophy'.[59] Furthermore, such a news organ should inform anthroposophists all over the world about the progress of spiritual-scientific research activity in Dornach; i.e., about the further unfolding of the 'being Anthroposophia'. According to Rudolf Steiner, members of the Anthroposophical Society should have, or rediscover, an interest and understanding '*of all things pertaining to the development of anthroposophy itself*'.[60] The news organ conceived by Rudolf Steiner in 1923 should contain not only essential news from the different countries, but also from Dornach itself, with regard to general anthroposophy and its specific professional projects, which were represented in lectures and courses. According to Rudolf Steiner, it would be possible in this way to develop and consequently strengthen the Anthroposophical Society as a worldwide active ideal and spiritual context.

★

As is known, Rudolf Steiner's efforts in reorganizing the Anthroposophical Society did not play out in a featureless period, but in a restricted, dangerous time. Rudolf Steiner was not only connected in a loving way to the social relationships developed as of 1902, but knew how essential he could be in the future for the anthroposophical work regarding civilization as a whole—and this in just such a difficult and tense time-period. In view of the unforeseeable and ever-mounting, anti-democratic, nationalistic forces and tendencies in Germany and various other European countries, which heralded an epoch of Totalitarianism or Fascism, a close, internationally functioning anthroposophical cooperation was definitely imperative—as long as one wanted to be further effective under difficult conditions in the coming years. Economically, Germany quickly became impoverished and its entire anthroposophical institutions were threatened financially; moreover, the political radicalization was foreseeable. Just one-and-a-half years before Hitler's first attempted putsch in Munich, Rudolf Hess, later his proxy, won a competition in summer 1922 on the theme 'What characteristics will a person have who leads Germany forward?' in which he described Hitler's personality indirectly and concluded with the statement: 'Thus, we have the picture of the dictator: full of spirit, clear and true, passionate and yet controlled, cold and daring, determined and balanced in making decisions, unrestrained in quick enforcement, ruthless towards himself and others, mercilessly tough and yet tender in love for his folk, untiring at work, with iron fist in velvet glove, capable, finally conquering himself. Still we do not know when he, the "man", will come to the rescue. But millions believe that he will come . . .'[61] Rainer Maria Rilke wrote at the beginning of 1923 in several letters from Switzerland about his fear regarding Germany's dangerous—and the world's endangered—future: *'for me [. . .] there is no doubt that it is Germany which, in so far as it does not understand itself, detains the world'*.[62] Inasmuch as Rudolf Steiner began in 1923 to move the organizational and spiritual centre of anthroposophy out of Germany and into Switzerland, and—associated with this—also into various other countries, he took these circumstances into account. The development of anthroposophical spiritual science was always closely connected with the philosophy of German idealism and the spirituality of Germany; however, under the then-present circumstances, in which this country continued to distance itself from its true inner nature, very little was possible.

At the end of 1923 Rudolf Steiner finally founded the Anthroposophical Society anew as the 'General Anthroposophical Society' in Dornach, as well as the School of Spiritual Science—and assumed the chairmanship of the Society and the esoteric leadership of the School. Ita Wegman wrote, among other things, about the difficult months preceding these decisions:

> Rudolf Steiner was always looking for solutions that could bring about a change [in the Anthroposophical Society]. He was deeply distressed. Courses in Penmaenmawr and Ilkley took place [in the summer of] 1923. And it seemed to me as though from this moment on Rudolf Steiner was thinking of a solution. He spoke about how the scorching fire that destroyed the first Goetheanum had revealed mighty secrets that gradually became clear to him in an overall picture. Mystery wisdom has been freed and this Mystery wisdom, which was guarded in various earlier Mysteries, should now become the good teachings of anthroposophy. The Society must, however, be reorganized. In this regard, Rudolf Steiner no longer said that the Society [...] should receive a new impulse, but rather he spoke of a new organization. Rudolf Steiner spoke these words after the trip to England. There arose a great activity in Rudolf Steiner's being. It was as if he could not start working fast and thoroughly enough for the changes.[63]

The connections and Mystery-background indicated in abbreviated form by Ita Wegman were complex.[64] Finally, Rudolf Steiner decided to personally take on the guidance and reorganization of the Anthroposophical Society, because he had seen in activities throughout the years that no rigorous, promising and committed reform-initiatives were forthcoming from the ranks of leading personalities; instead there was considerable misunderstanding of his real intentions. If Rudolf Steiner wanted to adhere to the goal of the Anthroposophical Society being an essential, effective instrument for anthroposophy, he had to newly form this Society himself, with a few co-workers whom he knew understood his intentions. Among these people was above all Ita Wegman, who had grasped Rudolf Steiner's will for change early on and had long since seen and regretted the Anthroposophical Society's weaknesses. According to her, Rudolf Steiner decided at the end of November 1923 to personally assume chairmanship of the 'General Anthroposophical Society', which was being created. To the Stuttgart branch-director Toni Völker, who continually had a tense relationship with Carl Unger and wanted to present new suggestions at the Christmas Conference in the Goetheanum, Ita Wegman wrote the following on 2 December 1923:

> This matter will be handled differently than hitherto with the founding of the individual national Societies. It is now Dr Steiner who wishes to take the entire matter into his hands; he will even be the leading chairman and direct the entire matter in the way he feels is right. He will also issue the statutes, and the legalities of the international Society will be conducted under his direct guidance, with the help of co-workers who live here in Dornach and are personally selected by him. Suggestions from others are now entirely out of the question; the national Societies simply have the option to join or not to join, and need only concern themselves with the question of yes or no.[65]

Three weeks later, still before the beginning of the Christmas Conference, Rudolf Steiner said in a Dornach lecture:

> This organization will now have to be such, my dear friends, that this Anthroposophical Society fulfils the conditions that simply arise out of present-day circumstances. And I must say that this Christmas Conference must occur in such a way that one can promise of it: Now an effective and capable Anthroposophical Society will emerge. I must already say that should this intention not be fulfilled, then I would indeed be compelled to bear every consequence—a fact of which I have spoken repeatedly.[66]

According to Rudolf Steiner, 'something must be created' through the Christmas Conference and with the new foundation of the General Anthroposophical Society, 'which, simply through the way it exists, is real'.[67] What followed in the succeeding days has been repeatedly described and spiritually illuminated in the last decades[68]—Rudolf Steiner personally took over the chairmanship of the Anthroposophical Society and created the conditions for further work, *'for promoting, for developing, for fully unfolding the Anthroposophical Society'*.[69] He assumed full responsibility for the future of the Anthroposophical World-Society and wanted to bring to light how anthroposophy should be represented in the world in the future—also, and primarily, with regard to young people.

In this way, the history of the Anthroposophical Society actually began anew—with a centre that was no longer in Stuttgart, but in Switzerland, at the Goetheanum, and whose new development Rudolf Steiner managed with increased strength. At the Goetheanum, the *'soul of the Anthroposophical Movement'* should be found in the future;[70] from there the General Anthroposophical Society should be directed, from now on, by Rudolf Steiner and the co-workers of his 'esoteric Council'; by people 'with initiative for the anthroposophical cause',[71] to which the 'real, actual guidance of the anthroposophical cause' would be given.[72] Undoubtedly, in the centre of the new organization was Rudolf Steiner, who not only directed the General Anthroposophical Society, but also the School of Spiritual Science ('... that the School of Spiritual Science at the Goetheanum in Dornach, with respect to all esotericism, will be directed by me'[73]). Rudolf Steiner's Council-colleagues were all at the same time Section leaders, i.e., people with ('through') whose help he wanted to lead and further develop the School in professional fields in the future. The professional work in connection with the existing medical, pedagogical, therapeutic, natural-scientific, artistic, social and religious organizations and institutions should belong to the core of the new General Anthroposophical Society; thereby the first of two cardinal problems of the Society should be solved (or a solution found) of which Rudolf Steiner always spoke in 1923. At the same time, anthroposophy as such should be further intensified and internalized by the members. Rudolf Steiner spoke about a Foundation Stone being laid in the hearts of the members—as well as the fact that the Michaelic spirituality of anthroposophy must in the future penetrate the Anthroposophical Society in a new way, as long as it wishes to continue to exist. ('Only when in this way we can bring the Anthroposophical Movement into ourselves as our *deepest heartfelt concern* will the Anthroposophical Society exist. When we cannot do that, it will not exist.'[74]) According to Rudolf Steiner, the 'spiritual–esoteric' should in the future be the basis and foundation of *all* work in the Society—provided with impulses by the Dornach researchers and the reality of the School, which Rudolf Steiner impressively brought to portrayal. The School of Spiritual Science directed by him will, said Rudolf Steiner, take care that 'esoteric life may once again flow into our Anthroposophical Society'[75] and in this way gradually make the 'intentions' of the Christmas Conference a reality.

★

Rudolf Steiner understood the new foundation of the Anthroposophical Society and its School—which he consummated through a spiritual–

esoteric act—as the beginning of a new development, in accordance with what he had outlined again and again in the months after the fire. This development could only be successful if the members grasped and worked with him on the process of deep-rooted transformation. The Christmas Conference should bring a 'new impulse' into the Anthroposophical Society—in seizing the exoteric world-responsibility, and in a much more advanced esoteric deepening of anthroposophy than ever before: '*We must be clear that especially our Society will have the task of combining the greatest conceivable openness with genuine, true esotericism.*'[76] Much, if not all, depended on the sufficient understanding of this task among the members—in a time when the momentous character of what was being decided for civilization was apparent. ('Very much, an enormous amount, is presently being decided for humanity.'[77]) The Christmas Conference should illuminate a new epoch, with much 'stronger impetus', in the history of the Anthroposophical Society.[78] 'The consciousness of this new impulse cannot be encouraged enough.'[79] In the weeks and months after the conference, Rudolf Steiner continually emphasized how important the intended intensification of anthroposophy actually was for perceiving its 'worldly' responsibility and its real internalization within the Anthroposophical Society. ('*Esotericism is based on the [...] internalization of the communication of truths. One should see in this internalization something of the impulse that the Christmas Conference intended to bring into the Anthroposophical Society.*'[80]) Rudolf Steiner expected uncompromising further work out of the spiritual centre of modern, Michaelic spiritual science and wanted everything that proceeded from Dornach to assume the character of this impulse. ('*What should be an impetus in the correct way, what should now proceed from Dornach—this must [...] be an impulse that does not come from the Earth, but an impulse that has its source in the spiritual world. We want to develop here the strength to follow impulses out of the spiritual world.*'[81]) Anthroposophy should continue to be taught extensively, unfolded in civilization with decisiveness and placed ever more in the centre; but it should be the 'internalization' of spiritual-scientific content, its meditative-esoteric penetration and thereby its connection with the innermost kernel of receptive people, that serves as a prerequisite for our comprehensive activities. Only by continually developing inner substance and only by cultivating this spiritual–esoteric foundation in 'all our activity and being'[82] can, Rudolf Steiner says, 'the future effectiveness of anthroposophy come about for civilization—in medicine and education, in agriculture and art, in religion and social life'. With complete decisiveness

Rudolf Steiner pointed out right at the beginning of the Christmas Conference that it would, from now on, be a matter of working directly, openly and in an undisguised way for anthroposophy; and he said straight away in his opening lecture at the conference:

> Whatever the realm, we must stand in the world under the sign of the full truth as representatives of the essence of anthroposophy. We must be aware that if we are incapable of doing so we cannot actually further the aims of the Anthroposophical Movement. Any veiled representation of the Anthroposophical Movement leads in the end to no good.[83]

Soon after this he added:

> If we ask ourselves over and over again what we must do to make ourselves better-liked by this or that circle in the world, by any circle which does not like us today; if we keep asking ourselves how we should behave in this field or in that field so as to be taken seriously here or there; if we do this, we shall most certainly not be taken seriously. We shall only be taken seriously if at every moment, in whatever we do, we feel responsible towards the spiritual world. We must know that the spiritual world wants to achieve a certain development with mankind at this particular moment in historical evolution; it wants to achieve this in the most varied realms of life, and it is up to us clearly and truly to follow the impulses that come from the spiritual world. Though this might give offence initially, in the long run it is the only beneficial way. Therefore we shall also only come to terms among ourselves if at every opportunity we steep ourselves in what can come as an impulse from the spiritual world.[84]

Four weeks before the beginning of the Christmas Conference, the director at that time of ILAG, later Weleda, wrote to Rudolf Steiner: 'In view of our great competition at the present time, in order to successfully market our preparations, the idea must be placed temporarily in the background. The preparations must not be advertised as coming from anthroposophical science, but must be placed on the market only as successful new medicines and specialties, otherwise we will never reach a broad audience and the medical institutions will also react dismissively.'[85]
To such a procedure and position Rudolf Steiner gave an absolutely clear and significant rejection at the Christmas Conference:

Yet anthroposophy will quite definitely remain unfruitful in the realm of medicine, especially therapy, if the tendency persists to represent matters within the field of medicine in the Anthroposophical Movement in a manner that anthroposophy as such is pushed into the background, so as to meet with the approval of those who represent medicine in the ordinary way today. We must carry anthroposophy courageously into every realm, including medicine.[86]

Rudolf Steiner intended that *only* anthroposophy and nothing else will be taught in Dornach and carried into the world from Dornach in the future: 'In the future, in the various areas of life, we will operate sincerely and honestly for anthroposophy from here, from Dornach, in full openness. Then people will also know for what they are giving their money.'[87]

★

Rudolf Steiner worked further until his death on what he had begun with the Christmas Conference, for the Anthroposophical Society and the School of Spiritual Science in Dornach. He prepared the construction of the second building and worked intensively together with all Section leaders in their respective professional area—in the Arlesheim Clinic, in preparing the artistic presentations in Dornach (and other places), in publications or supporting textbooks and monographs (with Ita Wegman, Günther Wachsmuth and Elisabeth Vreede), in developing the biodynamic agriculture, in his incessant dedication to the Waldorf School, in his cooperation with Albert Steffen for the weekly newsletter and newsorgan of the General Anthroposophical Society, which was so dear to his heart—and in many other areas of activity. In the area of medicine it was possible for Rudolf Steiner to hold two professional courses based on mantras for young doctors, which demonstrated how the esoteric content of the School of Spiritual Science would be realized in the context of specific professions; but also School-related courses and lectures for priests, teachers, therapeutic workers, farmers and artists took place 1924 within the individual professional areas of the School of Spiritual Science. Around these courses there formed the first professional communities of a spiritual orientation—this belonged to the inner core of what was envisioned for the Sections in Dornach.[88]

As the fundamental esoteric course of the School, Rudolf Steiner opened the 'First Class' in mid-February 1924, which took place within the General Anthroposophical Society and was intended equally for all professional groups; it represented the spirituality of the School in the sense of a systematic path of training. In addition, Rudolf Steiner held over 80 karma lectures for members of the General Anthroposophical Society, which belonged to the centre of his anthroposophic work, and the special task of which lay in further illuminating the background of the Anthroposophical Movement's destiny—thus they also constituted a fundamental contribution to further unfolding and deepening the General Anthroposophical Society. Finally, Rudolf Steiner composed regularly appearing *Letters to the Members* and *Leading Thoughts* for the anthroposophical work of individual groups and branches. In them, he reported about his work for anthroposophy in Dornach and other European cities; i.e., he described the content of the courses and lectures he gave, as well as conferences that were held, in accord with his intention for the newsletter *What Is Happening in the Anthroposophical Society?*, about which he had repeatedly spoken in the course of 1923 and at the Christmas Conference. Together with the *Leading Thoughts*, Rudolf Steiner's letters followed the intention 'of raising the entire membership to a common consciousness of the being of the Anthroposophical Society'[89]; i.e., they served to encourage 'consolidation and positive work' within the Society. Rudolf Steiner considered the *Leading Thoughts* issued from the Goetheanum as 'stimulation', and hoped that their content would be further deepened in individual study groups based on 'anthroposophical books and lecture-cycle literature'; i.e., with the help of the short *Leading Thoughts* essays, he intended to encourage Society members to deal intensively with the literature already printed in his spiritual-scientific basic books and lecture courses. 'There is presently a real science of the spiritual world that has been compiled over the years, and in important particulars already published', emphasized Rudolf Steiner, especially in the statutes of the Christmas Conference (and on other occasions).[90] He then wrote, additionally: '*One should not underestimate the work that has already been accomplished in the Anthroposophical Society and which is available in the published cycles and lectures.*'[91] With the quintessence of the *Leading Thoughts* and the study work made possible by them, Rudolf Steiner hoped to help 'the available literature gradually to become the spiritual property of the membership'[92] through a new and more intensive study of the original anthroposophy. He knew how much depended upon whether the future formation of the General Anthroposophical Society into a spiritual organization would really succeed. This development and thereby the 'identity' of the Society, however, depended on the real reception of anthroposophy. When mentioning reception, through which the results of anthroposophical spiritual research could become the 'spiritual property' of the members, Rudolf Steiner meant not the simple hearing or reading of corresponding lectures and books, but the actual absorption of the essential anthroposophy into the 'living soul nature' of the individual and the Society. Anthroposophy is, he wrote in his *Letters to Members*, not only a 'spiritual-scientific system of knowledge' but also 'something living in the hearts of many people'.[93] He characterized the 'further thinking' and 'further feeling' of the spiritual-scientific content as a methodical path for developing one's own point of view—precisely this process should be supported by studying the *Leading Thoughts* (and the considerations connected with them). Anthroposophy should finally become '*true life*' ('True life is its nature'[94])—and this 'life' should continue to be at work in an intensive manner in the Anthroposophical Society. In it and through it the being of Anthroposophy should be able to reveal itself. From the leading anthroposophists, who held lectures themselves, Rudolf Steiner expected, even required, that their representations no longer be intellectual-theoretical and generally of an abstract nature, but directly full of life, in heart-felt warmth and thought-light. '*Anthroposophical truths are, from a certain point of view, the most important that people can communicate. To convey such information to another without bringing about a deep inner interest in what is said is actually a misrepresentation of it.*'[95] Rudolf Steiner hoped for a 'fundamental attitude of love' and an experiential 'respect for the spiritual life' in all anthroposophical lectures, public as well as internal; and moreover, a special 'potency', about which he wrote in a further statement:

> As to this element of potency—we should never try to bring it by external means into our talk on anthroposophy. We should just let it evolve out of the living feeling which we have towards the truths of anthroposophy, realising that as we grasp them in our soul we approach the reality of the spiritual world. This will give a certain mood to our soul; for certain moments, our soul will feel itself absolutely given up to thoughts of the spiritual world. In such moments the reverence for the spiritual is born in a perfectly natural and unconstrained way. The beginning of all true meditation lies in the development of such a mood. Whoever is unable to love this

mood of soul will apply in vain the rules for attaining knowledge of a 'spiritual world'. For it is in this mood that the spiritual, which lives in the depths of the human soul, is called into consciousness. A person thereby unites himself with his own spiritual being. And only in this union can he find the spiritual in the world. Only the spiritual in the human being can approach the spiritual in the world.[96]

In this way Rudolf Steiner worked until his death on 30 March 1925, not only on making the General Anthroposophical Society an efficient working organ for anthroposophy and its individual foundations in the world, but also on developing its unique spirituality and social being, its 'identity'—*through the substance of anthroposophy.*

Completion-ceremony of the second Goetheanum building, Dornach, 29 September 1926

2. The Challenges of the Present and Future

Lecture: Dornach, 30 March 2012

'Try to grow together with the world! That will be the best and most important "programme". Of course, this cannot be put into the statutes; it is something we should be able to instil into our hearts like a flame!'

Rudolf Steiner[97]

Dear friends,

The year 2011, lying behind us, was an exoteric year for anthroposophy in a quite positive sense. Never before has Rudolf Steiner and his work been perceived to such an extent in the world, through the numerous events, articles and books. The question of the relation to Rudolf Steiner and anthroposophy was discussed intensively within the Anthroposophical Society. 'What is our relationship to Rudolf Steiner today?' Much indicates that 2012 must be an esoteric year, a year of deepening into the being of Anthroposophy and everything connected with her. In paraphrasing a formulation by Hans Mayers, the great literary scientist who is now deceased, I think that the decisive, internal–esoteric question for the Anthroposophical Society must henceforth be as follows: 'How do we stand *before* Rudolf Steiner today?' This means: not only our position with regard to him, but specifically our being in front of him—face to face with his spiritual form, and in view of what he and his work expect, hope and require from us.

Looking back at the preceding 20th century from our present perspective, we can see that it was a period of immeasurable destruction—of widespread attempted and realized destruction of people as human entities, as well as of the basis for our life on Earth. This could be expanded and explained in detail, which is however not our task here and now. Instead, it is essential to note that today, looking back upon the entire century, it is without doubt easier and more possible now than it was in 1923/24 to see what Rudolf Steiner really supported with his anthroposophy; what he was for and what he was against. When Rudolf Steiner said in 1923 that the spiritual truths of anthroposophical spiritual science '*only and alone are able truly to elevate human dignity*',[98] then for us this is particularly comprehensible after the fact, especially in view of the contrast [which has become manifest in the time since]. It is clear to us what consequences the materialistic human image have had, how consistently Fascist totalitarianism, as well as genocide and euthanasia, were built upon this human image. The so-called 'extermination of all unworthy life' initiated in the 20th century had its clear thought-foundation, which in the end also took hold of people's feeling and will—precisely as Rudolf Steiner wrote in anticipating this in November 1924, in his essay 'The World-Thoughts in the Activity of Michael and in the Working of Ahriman'.[99] Based on what was happening in the form of evil and destructive activity, which worked to overshadow the real human image, we can now see more clearly in a reflection and overview of the century the importance of anthroposophy and its complete understanding of humanity and the cosmos. Only the spiritual-scientific points of view are, Rudolf Steiner emphasized in 1923, really in a position '*to bring peace over the Earth once again*'.[100] For us today, this is at least likely to be understandable—clearer and more definite than it was for the people who had heard Rudolf Steiner speaking publicly and internally, in the inner space of the Anthroposophical Society of his time. With Rudolf Steiner's summons to grasp 'the prosperity of the anthroposophical matter as an affair of present-day civilization',[101] many members were more or less helpless and overtaxed. Today, however, we can see that what was connected with Rudolf Steiner's appearance and activity actually represented once more a decisive attempt to change things—or better said, to change world processes; and this largely in the attempted healing of the Earth which was threatened by unspeakable catastrophes in the realms of politics, social life and all of civilization, including ecology. 'Where there is danger, there increases / The potential for salvation as well',[102] wrote Hölderlin, just having become ill, in his Patmos-Hymn of 1804—and Bruno Walter, the outstanding musician, understood Rudolf Steiner's anthroposophy in this way: 'Here lives and works this force for salvation in Hölderlin's sense ...'[103]

When we look back, we must however—despite our positive words about the year 2011—also observe that anthroposophy as a whole is not pervasive. The over 1,000 Waldorf Schools, which have in the meantime been founded all over the world, cannot change our minds about this. If one occupies oneself more deeply and precisely with Rudolf Steiner's life-work, follows his individual paths and intentions in detail—and enters into his 'collected works' not just as a quarry of interesting 'stimulations'—it becomes clear that most of what Rudolf Steiner proposed, prepared and put into operation, using all his life-forces in the process, has failed in the 20th century. The situation of the Prologue to the Gospel of St John appears on the horizon, the idea of the light that shines in the darkness, but has not been received by this darkness. Inasmuch as we here, in the Goetheanum, in the internal setting of the Anthroposophical Society, think about this situation, we must ask ourselves to what extent we have contributed to this tragedy, and continue to do so. It is too easy, too simple—and in the end also a distortion of the truth—to attribute the rejection of anthroposophy as a whole, in the context of our entire Society, only to adverse environmental circumstances, to obstacles and to the prevailing thought-paradigms of our scientists, politicians, theologians and publicists, who, as everybody knows, have made life difficult and have further complicated things for anthroposophy. The image of a 'hostile world' is too simple, and as member of the Anthroposophical Society one must also ask to what an extent this Society was and is a suitable instrument for disseminating anthroposophy—that is, for spreading the anthroposophy of Rudolf Steiner. This notorious blaming of the 'outer world' leads us away from what lies in the area of our own responsibility. Ita Wegman described Rudolf Steiner's anthroposophy as a 'powerful gift', but also said: '*And there arises ever and again the question: Have we become worthy of it?*'[104] On this basis, I believe, the question posed about the 'identity' of the Anthroposophical Society is an urgent one: It is not only intellectually interesting and worth considering, but harbours an existential element connected with our existence and non-existence as a Society. 'How do we stand *before* Rudolf Steiner?' That also means: What have we done for his work, for its comprehension and recognition, for its helpful introduction into civilization?

Most of us who are gathered here in the Goetheanum at this hour—on the anniversary of Rudolf Steiner's death—will in a few years or decades have to appear before Rudolf Steiner's figure in the spiritual world. The question posed at the beginning, 'How do we stand *before* Rudolf Steiner today?', will then, at the very latest, become practical and concrete. But it can also be so before our earthly death: through inner meditations as well as through many situations in our life and work. It is not a question that one can advance and pose publicly in a meaningful way, not a question of modern journalism and of our contemporary newspapers. It is however, in my conviction, a *question of the life* of the Anthroposophical Society which we cannot avoid, even though we attempt to do so constantly.

What did Rudolf Steiner expect from members of the Anthroposophical Society after 30 March 1925? We don't know and—without self-overestimation—cannot say. But we can, as an initial approximation, ask his students—those who have actually experienced this crossing of the threshold, remained connected with Rudolf Steiner esoterically and lived with this question. Among these spiritually developed and awakened people is undoubtedly Michael Bauer, whom I want to remember here on the anniversary of Rudolf Steiner's death. It is known that Michael Bauer was beyond reproach concerning all of the Society's doubts and conflicts, and acted during Rudolf Steiner's life as one of his esoteric master-pupils. The Anthroposophical Society, in whose board of directors he served until his illness, was a central concern of his; and after his teacher's death, he wrote several essays regarding this Society—its being and the next tasks belonging to its internal identity.[105] One of the first and most urgent tasks of the General Anthroposophical Society that Michael Bauer described at this time was to bring Rudolf Steiner's image, the spiritual scientist and man, truthfully into culture, i.e., to make it possible for future generations to find Rudolf Steiner. Regarding this Michael Bauer wrote, among other things, the following:

> A tremendous amount can be accomplished when the discouraging prejudices and also the superstitions about the person Rudolf Steiner are overcome. For many people are not able to break out of this spell of the times. They need *help*, for which they are fundamentally looking.
>
> Perhaps many of the older generation sought Rudolf Steiner's work, because they were not able to deal with the pressure of their lives or found no satisfaction in any other way: *Now* the time has come to carry forward and disseminate his work out of a *free decision*—for the sake of those seeking, yearning in view of the great *needs* of our time.[106]

Like Marie Steiner and Ita Wegman, Michael Bauer was of the view that Rudolf Steiner's greatness was underestimated by his contemporaries, also by his closest co-workers and students. '*We are standing too close*', he wrote with wonderful simplicity in one of his letters.[107] Actually, there often exists among us the hasty opinion that Rudolf Steiner's anthroposophical contemporaries knew him best. This is however highly questionable, even as the possibility of personal meetings, conversations, listening to his lecturers, etc., would have been of singular importance—which Andrei Belyi witnessed most impressively. Still, Michael Bauer was right: The historical centennial-retrospect now possible, and also the existing complete edition of Rudolf Steiner's work, including many individual documents from his biography, make possible for us today an access to his being which was not so readily available for the contemporaries 'in the darkness of the experienced moment'—to cite Ernst Bloch. But also, I believe, we still stand 'too close'; one often has that impression. As long as the Earth and mankind still have a future, then I think our view of Rudolf Steiner will have an entirely different urgency and form in a few centuries than it does today. I personally do not think interest in the biography and being of Rudolf Steiner will subside in the future; nor do I think that anthroposophy will be active in such a way as can be read about in some anthroposophical journals of 2011/12. I believe that the opposite will be true—and later centuries will be surprised at how carelessly the General Anthroposophical Society in our time had often dealt with this singular Initiate and his work, his literary and artistic estates, his statements and intentions—which in the present are apparently little studied and penetrated by opinion-forming personalities, and are often even allowed to fall into obscurity. I would like here to call to mind what the great artist Assya Turgenieff said in exemplary manner in the mid-1950s, as she defended herself in vain against a reconstruction plan for the Goetheanum that did not correspond to Rudolf Steiner's artistic intentions: 'In other places, one excavates old cultural structures ... Here we cover up the form and arrangement that Dr Steiner gave to us for the Mystery-space of the present time ...'[108] 'Who really has the competence for remodelling the Goetheanum? It shows that there is no clarity any more. Since Rudolf Steiner's death, the relationships among the School of Spiritual Science, the Goetheanum administration, the Executive Council and the Society are ever more confused. If in the course of 33 years an impulse has not been understood and developed enough, then according to Rudolf Steiner it turns into something entirely different. This applies to the Constitution of the Society as well as the renovation of the Goetheanum, and the one is connected with the other. A thorough study of the Constitution of the Society and the School of Spiritual Science should be undertaken *in all circles of the Anthroposophical Movement* and a complete study of all documents for remodelling the Goetheanum should precede this development.'[109]

★

Let us return to Michael Bauer once again. He spoke about the task of the General Anthroposophical Society: that of developing the true image of

Rudolf Steiner for the sake of those people who are seeking—people who, in view of the 'great needs of our time', are looking for orientation, help and new beginnings. In other places, Michael Bauer also wrote that it is 'our task [...] to continually bring the work in our consciousness into confrontation with the *terrible needs of the time*, so that it will remain living...'[110] One could also say that it is our task to allow the School of Spiritual Science in Dornach to become real, with all its Sections, which develop anthroposophy's contribution to the 'terrible needs of our time' and which have the potential to transform our time, even if only to a limited extent.

I want to discuss these two themes that Michael Bauer wrote about, and which to him belonged to the central identity of the Anthroposophical Society. Naturally, the well-known, all-too-familiar argument can follow that Michael Bauer's access to the tasks of the Anthroposophical Society belonged to the 1920s of the previous century, and does not apply at all to present-day standards. Whether this is really so, I would venture to doubt. It is undeniable that much has changed in the world since 1925, and much in a serious way; these changes, however, did not come as a surprise, but lay and lie within the logic of the forces that already determined the beginning of the 20th century's historical events; this could be documented in detail. Rudolf Steiner responded to these forces with the initiation-science of anthroposophy, and with the founding of the Anthroposophical Movement and Society. He did not conduct anthroposophical research for merely a few years, nor did he establish the Goetheanum as a School of Spiritual Science for a short, provisional time-period. Rudolf Steiner consummated the Christmas Conference almost as if he was himself a participant—and he knew the time remaining for him on Earth would possibly be quite short. Moreover, his assessment at the end of 1923, brought to expression extensively in his stated objectives, was meant for the future—for a time-period that we have still in no way outlived or gone beyond. If a person overlooks or misjudges, denies or reduces all this, he misunderstands—in my view—Rudolf Steiner and anthroposophy, and finds himself caught in a tragic error. However, let us go back to Rudolf Seiner's 'image' and the General Anthroposophical Society.

As is known, the 'exoteric' year 2011, the 150th birthday of Rudolf Steiner, yielded—along with many successful events—also new biographies which have found great publicity and have had a strong impact. These publications were classified as 'authoritative works', and some were also positively reviewed or referred to in anthroposophical newsletters.

What would Michael Bauer have said about this? One cannot ask him, but it is also not necessary; in my view his answer is obvious—also in view of his morality and seriousness, his uncompromising, truthful nature. Miriam Gebhardt, qualified historian at the University of Konstanz, begins her biography with the sentence: 'Rudolf Steiner, founder of anthroposophy, could speak with the dead. They gave him a glimpse into their knowledge and he made their incarnations his business.'[111] This sentence is a flat lie— Rudolf Steiner never claimed he could make the incarnations of the dead his 'business' and he never—in exchange—received knowledge from them. Of course, Mrs Gebhardt did not at all mean that sincerely, but cynically. It is, however, the *first sentence* in her whole book in which Rudolf Steiner—in the course of the text—is represented as 'travelling salesman of self-produced truths'[112] and as 'guru for belief- and lifestyle-questions';[113] as a person who boasted 'an all-explaining worldview',[114] who was not at all an 'original thinker' but much more a 'successful populariser' of contemporary truths,[115] a swindler who 'managed' his positions cunningly and helped himself 'generously, as no other, from the department store of modern ideas'.[116] Rudolf Steiner was for Mrs Gebhardt a 'bulimic thinker and lecturer',[117] who employed 'mass-suggestion'[118] and used astonishing strategies of 'self-dramatization' and 'self-marketing'.[119] And so forth. I think we can and must, as the General Anthroposophical Society, ask ourselves how we reacted to these targeted lies last year—to effective lies that have emphatically and momentously undermined the reputation of anthroposophy and Rudolf Steiner among broad portions of the population, and especially in academic circles. We do not need to ask how the community of the Dominicans in the 13th century, who also had a 'School of Spiritual Science', reacted to the corresponding 'biographies' of Thomas Aquinas—as a community order and school. Rather, we already have clear statements from Rudolf Steiner regarding how he hoped for such matters to be answered—and to be sure, he hoped for this not merely from individual fighters among anthroposophists, who were indeed to be found in 1923 (as well as 2011), and who defended him with all their energy, but from the General Anthroposophical Society and its leadership. Rudolf Steiner wanted and expected—and this is entirely justified!—that the Society would take action in such situations, take a position, and make the extent of the lies known courageously and directly. He expressed himself sharply in 1923 regarding all attempts to seek 'dialogue' with those who systematically distort and caricature anthroposophy—and to anthroposophical newsletters that give space to these people: 'We no longer need enemies for slander: for this we have our own newsletters', he said.[120] What would Rudolf Steiner have said about the fact that Helmut Zander's books are well-displayed and sold in a profitable manner within the Goetheanum? He would have closed that book store and dismissed all responsible persons—in my view, there is no way around this conclusion. It is logical. Conversely, it is also consistent that untruthful publications by Zander and similar authors would indeed be sold here in the Goetheanum when one is oneself convinced that the Anthroposophical Movement no longer lives in the sense Rudolf Steiner intended—and that today it is only a matter of analyzing this Movement critically as an historical phenomenon, in open, intellectual discourse. It is therefore, I think, a matter of existence or non-existence. One doesn't need a 'School of Spiritual Science' when one is not willing or able to represent—and if necessary, to defend—this spiritual science as such, in its reality. This defence does not involve 'sectarian', exclusive behaviour; quite to the contrary. Rudolf Steiner was a person open to the world: a contemporary in the true sense of the word. This, however, does not mean that one fawns over people who distort anthroposophical concerns beyond recognition and who represent Rudolf Steiner in a dishonourable way—people who not only represent a shift in perspective, but who operate on the lowest moral (and literary) level. In my opinion, it is an attempt at extermination, a sort of murdering of the spiritual being of a person—a process that one should consider in a Kaspar Hauser year. How was this noble spirit and martyr treated, and how will he be treated? But besides Kaspar Hauser and his destiny—what native site, or rather, which *work place* of Hegel, Albert Schweitzer or Mahatma Gandhi would think of selling such abusive publications in their own facility? If a person treads this path, he associates not only the concerns of Rudolf Steiner and Michael Bauer with their grotesque opposite, but removes himself from anthroposophy in a way that, a few decades ago, would have been unthinkable—and undoubtedly shows signs of an agony, medically stated; of a dissolution and dying process whose symptoms are manifold. In his narration of *The Fifth Gospel*, Rudolf Steiner spoke in an exemplary way about the nature and the pathogenic—in reality *morbid*—effect of a fallen, once-existing but then alienated Mystery centre. It is worth reading these statements and relating them not only to Palestine and a former Mithras-cult centre 2,000 years ago. I take it that Rudolf Steiner didn't go into such detail about this place for nothing.

Let us return, however, to the positive, to the absolutely positive. Like

Michael Bauer, I am of the opinion that for the General Anthroposophical Society it is a matter of allowing Rudolf Steiner's spiritual form and intentional concerns to become visible, to represent *him* and *his work*. '*I am here as representative of the anthroposophy proceeding from the Goetheanum . . .*'[121] Further, it is a matter of continually 'bringing the work in our consciousness into confrontation with the terrible needs of the time'; i.e., developing and further strengthening the School of Spiritual Science in its professional Sections. Their successes are, I believe, very considerable. If a person writes the history of anthroposophy and the Goetheanum as a School of Spiritual Science, it would be impressive to represent what contents and perspectives from the Goetheanum have transformed the world in the previous decades, what concrete work has been accomplished and what human relationships have formed—around a professional scope of tasks, in the realms of medicine, agriculture, education, therapy, natural science and art; also in the area of religion in so far as this is further represented through the 'Movement for Religious Renewal', the Christian Community. For the General Anthroposophical Society, however, there is the task of supporting these activities with energy—by really taking part in them, through personal engagement *and* by maintaining the esoteric core of anthroposophy in the Society itself. Rudolf Steiner never allowed us to doubt that general anthroposophy needed productive spirituality in the work, which can be experienced in the professional areas; i.e., which are not only taken for granted as given and 'known', but continually internalized actively and meditatively. It is often underestimated in our contemporary anthroposophical setting just how comprehensive and detailed Rudolf Steiner's spiritual-scientific research results really are—in various areas of life and in general human and cosmic insight, in historical and spiritual knowledge. It is, as we know—and Rudolf Steiner was the first to become painfully aware of this—a 'diffuse' work, which is divided or 'scattered' into numerous lecture-courses, in forms of communication and discourse, which people followed not in a systematic manner, but with a specific quality of thought. We all know—or at least could know—that this is connected with the special conditions of Rudolf Steiner's life's work; and we can further know how much an overview of the individual statements made here or there meant to him. Over and over again, he challenged people unobtrusively to read the different cycles 'together'—or reacted full of joy when individual people were active in this way out of their own initiative. Every attempt of this kind is a contribution towards bringing the spiritual-scientific work— or more specifically, a spiritual-scientific research that exists singularly in the history of mankind—into visibility. This research is, however, the real basis of the School of Spiritual Science, which in my view cannot be doubted. We can and must, nearly nine decades after Rudolf Steiner's death, ask in Dornach: Why have we not succeeded, as Anthroposophical Society, to bring this work with its special nature and dignity, its scope and its differentiated forms, more competently into the world? It is absolutely not the case that the so-called 'world' is not interested in this life-work; on the contrary. What it lacks, I believe, is a selfless performance on our part. Anthroposophy still operates too much, and almost completely, as a study- and meditation-path for individuals or small groups. This work of individuals or communities is essentially and spiritually indispensable. Beyond that, however, Rudolf Steiner expected that colleagues would develop monographs and publications that apply to his spiritual-scientific research as such, and relate to their individual areas of application—as is unmistakeably shown by his statements in 1923/24. If a person continually attempts 'to bring the work in our consciousness into confrontation with the terrible needs of the time', two things are necessary: a real knowledge of the 'work'; i.e., the spiritual-science of Rudolf Steiner today promoted as anthroposophy, with its many statements and perspectives—*and* a real knowledge of the 'needs of the time': the contemporary questions of knowledge and life, with their difficulties, abysses and challenges. Rudolf Steiner hoped that the General Anthroposophical Society would take up this task and experience it as part of its inner identity. Repeatedly, he pointed out that anthroposophical spiritual science exists; i.e., that it has in many aspects been researched and made available. He wanted and hoped that it would be penetrated and internalized by the members of the Anthroposophical Society, and that this activity would be the condition for forming a new spiritual community with social effectiveness. Not the evasion of Rudolf Steiner, the indifference or the critical-minded apology for his being and his work—behind which are concealed forms of self-conscious relativization and detachment—but the real consummation of the process described is, I believe, the requirement of the hour and a vital aspect of anthroposophical identity. In the sense intended by Michael Bauer, this is a social assistance of the first order. In the words of Rudolf Steiner:

> One only advances forward when he represents the truth as strongly as possible, so that as many predestined souls as possible—who are present today in greater numbers than one generally supposes—come to find the spiritual nourishment that is necessary.[122]

The General Anthroposophical Society will be strengthened to the extent that this process succeeds; and with it, one day, also all the different institutions that were once connected with it but have predominantly lost this living connection, apart from a few exceptions. In my opinion, there can be no doubt about this. And Weleda, which is much-discussed at present, is only one of many companies which originally had a clear anthroposophical work-task—but which then made itself independent and went its own way, just as Rudolf Steiner spoke of warningly in 1923, and which became a reality at the latest through the social disruption of the 1930s. I think one should not, and must not, give way to illusions about the fact that this process, in its entirety, is not reversible. There are still many people who are authentically interested in nearly all anthroposophical institutions and initiatives. They are, as we know, not all members of the Anthroposophical Society. Why should they be? One can find anthroposophy outside the Society and esteem it—this Rudolf Steiner said impressively in 1923. Sometimes the Anthroposophical Society doesn't have an attractive effect—and what healthy young person is interested in time-consuming association meetings, statutes, Society disputes, officials, vanity and 'curule chairs'? After the burning of the Goetheanum, Rudolf Steiner spoke of an urgently needed 'positive momentum' in the Anthroposophical Society—and we all know that this process has still not succeeded sufficiently. Thus, the existential basis of the General Anthroposophical Society, as well as its 'inner identity', is more than questionable for many people: Who among us has no understanding for that?

The situation would be completely different if the General Anthroposophical Society could be experienced worldwide as an organization in which the esoteric core of anthroposophy, its real spirituality, lived powerfully; and if it also responsibly and effectively supported anthroposophical initiatives, schools, therapeutic homes, clinics and medical practices, farms, anthroposophical art and new social forms—and out of a special spirituality and humanity, took a public position regarding questions of preimplantation genetic diagnostics' and euthanasia, regarding genetic and bodily technology, and much more. As centre for the General Anthroposophical Society, the Goetheanum should become a 'cornerstone' and a '*protest building*', said Rudolf Steiner;[123] it should stand visibly and positively for a direction other than that of technological materialism, as well as initiating and supporting counter-developments to this dominant trend. To the extent that the Goetheanum fulfils this task, I believe, the General Anthroposophical Society will be interesting for many people at present and in the future. The 'courageous work out of the innermost core', of which Rudolf Steiner spoke, needs the spiritual structure of anthroposophy, and belongs to the most profound of what a person can experience in himself and others—together with others. The 'awakening to the soul-spiritual', of the other person, about which Rudolf Steiner spoke so impressively in 1923, is not a phenomenon of direct social meeting, but describes the mutual reception of original anthroposophy—and the recognition of how this anthroposophy lives in others.

The intensification of anthroposophy—understood in this way—within the Anthroposophical Society is therefore a central task of the future, and this is especially true here in the Dornach Goetheanum. From my point of view, the Goetheanum must be a place where in the future real anthroposophists from all over the world work—people for whom the esoteric core of anthroposophical spiritual science and the spiritual relationship to Rudolf Steiner is the central concern of their lives. The Goetheanum should invite these people to come and work with it in all the areas it represents. *Every* person who is active in this building—in whatever area and function—should, I believe, have a consciousness for the special quality of this Mystery-centre—should bring this with them, or at least acquire such a consciousness here. This is the way it was in Rudolf Steiner's lifetime—and so it could be again in the future, for there are correspondingly talented souls in the destiny of the Goetheanum, interested people worldwide who could assume co-responsibility in Dornach. Necessary and especially essential for the identity of the Anthroposophical Society is the creation or recovery of a place, which for the spiritual world—the dead, the unborn, coming souls and the Hierarchies—is interesting and important and therefore will be further *desired* and *supported* by them. This does not mean forming islands, but instead the vision or intention of a building where all co-workers take esoteric anthroposophy seriously—including its working into the world—and really know, affirm, and want the Goetheanum that was intended and prepared by Rudolf Steiner. As already emphasized—these people do exist and they could in the coming years and decades find their biographical way to Dornach *as long as* a real, radiating centre of anthroposophical spirituality again develops here—with general meetings, conferences and seminars that are the spiritual highlights of our lives. In the future, people who as anthroposophists have achieved a position in the world could also work in executive positions, and could combine this world-position with their colleagueship at the Goetheanum. The

Anthroposophical Society is not an end-in-itself and its own sole employer—and in the future its administration will very likely not be a full-time job. Diether Lauenstein, *as priest of the Christian Community*, once wanted to accept a respected and important professorship at the University of Tübingen—which was unfortunately denied to him by the 'Movement for Religious Renewal'. Dietrich Bonhoeffer encouraged that every evangelic minister complete a worldly career after World War II, in order not to lose sight of the encounter with social reality and thereby fall into a self-centred orientation. I am of the view that there is something of a future-oriented direction in these paths. I think it belongs to the identity of the Anthroposophical Society that it overcomes its fatal club-like nature, and finds a working form and structure suited to the 'needs of the time' and anthroposophy. The Society will have to examine how many time-consuming meetings and gatherings are really needed in order to be able to actually fulfil the tasks appointed or handed over by Rudolf Steiner. They will have to pose to themselves the question of efficiency, to critically examine their own committee-dynamics, also with regard to future appointment-procedures. If they want to be or become credible, from outside and inside, as a Society for anthroposophy, then they must overcome their bourgeois tendencies as well as all temptations to complacency and narcissism, to 'cults of personality', to journalistic photo-portraits, to intellectual vanity and to the exertion of power, especially in executive positions. One should not say that it is not possible for anthroposophical reasons—because the people simply are this way ... If a person postulates the limits of development, he thereby negates the very existential possibility of a Goetheanum and a real 'General Anthroposophical Society'. Rather, we can trust that the existential encounter with Rudolf Steiner's anthroposophy helps and advances one in this sense—at least *those* people who have 'goodwill'. The steps outlined above—all of which, I think, belong to the identity of an Anthroposophical Society worthy of this name—form the indispensable prerequisite for a real cooperation with and a real esteem for the achievements of others, of mutual support and encouragement, of which Rudolf Steiner spoke so intensively in 1923.

I come to the end and thereby back to the beginning. If a person reflects on the 20th century and especially on its first quarter, it is my opinion that much was still possible and open on a global scale then, which today (at least for the time being) must be considered as already negatively determined. Rudolf Steiner worked during a time which, in principle, allowed a totally different overarching direction to be found and embarked upon. This did not succeed and this task will also not be repeatable in this form—a fact that has consequences for the identity of the General Anthroposophical Society. 'In a different time period' and without an initiate like Rudolf Steiner in its ranks, I believe this Society cannot maintain *the* claim and *the* goals that it correctly formulated in the first quarter-century. The possibility of rescuing the world as a whole does not exist for us; we should have no illusions about this: Modesty is required instead of pathos and self-overestimation—also restraint with regard to advertisement and false pretences, which in the end are not redeemable and therefore deceptive. What at least can and must be continued is the fight for every human soul: every sick, needy, or 'handicapped' person; every square metre of living Earth; every new, future-oriented social form—and so forth. The exoteric-esoteric task given to the School of Spiritual Science still stands, and it can also be transformed, step-by-step, in mutual work and in spiritual connection with Rudolf Steiner's being. In this regard, the international character of the General Anthroposophical Society offers great possibilities, as we know and experience at all international Section-conferences; possibilities of cooperation and help, of comprehension and support. It should therefore also be possible in the future for the General Anthroposophical Society to find its way out of its crises and half-measures, and with determination, indeed to implement a new spiritual point of departure.

There is, however, no question that such a new point of departure requires the knowledge of its necessity; i.e., the insight that the Goetheanum cannot be maintained in its present form, and that an entirely different decisiveness for anthroposophy is needed at this place. In his poem 'Responsibility' Christian Morgenstern wrote:

> Here we are swaying idly back and forth—
> And above someone is waiting for us!
> Here we are swaying idly back and forth.
>
> In our loyalty lives no earnestness—
> And above someone is counting on us;
> In our loyalty works no earnestness.
>
> Neither above nor below gain
> Purpose and victory from such help.
> Thus, above and below develop

Shame and grief from such half-measures.
The gods on high starve and
Human beings wither. Bleak sorrow

Undermines the work of love in the world.[124]

I believe, however, that a corresponding turning point is possible. Thousands of members of the General Anthroposophical Society around the world want a real Goetheanum, a Goetheanum in the form Rudolf Steiner intended and prepared. In the future, it is hoped that these members will increasingly perceive and articulate their responsibility for this most central of Rudolf Steiner's foundations. For many other people, it is probably not possible at present to foresee what the existence of such a spiritually formed and effectively radiating place could mean to them, what a heartening influence it could have—lifted by impulses of the spiritual community of the General Anthroposophical Society to a high, spiritual–ethical level.

I am well aware that, for critics, it is highly questionable whether the General Anthroposophical Society—and with it the Goetheanum—really can be developed into such an organization in the future; many well regarded people with decades of prior experience and profound historical knowledge consider this to be ruled out completely, especially in view of all the accumulated grief in Dornach and the considerable guilt—both in a moral sense and with regard to the question of truth. Along with Willem Zeylmans van Emmichoven I would like to say personally: '*By no man will the General Anthroposophical Society be torn out of my heart!*'[125] I believe we should never forget that Rudolf Steiner was an 'optimist' all his life; we should never forget that anthroposophy is a resurrection science and that '*sincerity in love*' leads us further under any circumstances. In such an inner movement towards truth will the future, in principle, become visible; also the future of the General Anthroposophical Society, even if only in seed-form. On 8 February 1923, Rudolf Steiner said to a group of anthroposophical youth:

> You will have to suffer much. But even if anthroposophy were annihilated, it would rise up again, for it must do so, there is a need for it. Either the Earth has a future or it hasn't. The Earth's future is inseparable from anthroposophy. If anthroposophy has no future, mankind as a whole has no future either. *The tendency is alone sufficient.*[126]

The second Goetheanum

Appendix: The Relation to the School of Spiritual Science. Teachers, Doctors and Priests in 1924[127]

'In this sense, my dear friends, we want to remain united—we want to remain so united that you will keep the Goetheanum here in Dornach as your centre-point and really support this centre-point, so that this centre-point can work into the world through you.'

Rudolf Steiner[128]

In their first joint-meeting after the Christmas Conference and foundation of the School of Spiritual Science, the Stuttgart Waldorf teacher faculty convened with questions for Rudolf Steiner regarding the future relationship of the Waldorf School to the Goetheanum and the School of Spiritual Science. At this meeting, which took place in Stuttgart on 5 February 1924—ten days before the first Class Lesson—Rudolf Steiner made clear from the beginning that he didn't think a direct connection of the 'Free Waldorf School' to the Dornach School of Spiritual Science was favourable; rather, that 'the teacher faculty as such', '*or those personalities within the teacher faculty who desired—not only personally but as teachers of the Waldorf School*'—should join the School of Spiritual Science.[129] Joining the School in this fashion would bring about a 'living relationship', which would enable a mediation of the impulse from Dornach to the Waldorf School; Rudolf Steiner considered this desirable and necessary: 'The difference [in contrast to the status quo] was that formerly the relationship to anthroposophical education was more theoretical, and in the future it should become more active: In this sense, either the entire teacher faculty, or individual personalities, would focus on the impulses that result when one, as teacher of the Free Waldorf School, is a member of the School of Spiritual Science.'[130] At the time of the meeting—only five weeks after the Christmas Conference—most of the Stuttgart teachers had already applied for membership in the First Class and had written to Rudolf Steiner in Dornach in this regard. At the conference, Rudolf Steiner clarified that he not only thought it sensible and desirable for *all* teachers to apply to the Dornach School of Spiritual Science, which 'basically worked for insight and vitality', and in which individuals undertook 'learning in its essence' and at the same time could work together so that the School of Spiritual Science—as an academy—would really succeed in solving scientific and artistic problems;[131] he stipulated further that teachers become members not only as individual persons on their individual training-paths, but in their capacity *as teachers of the Stuttgart School*. Finally, he posed in express terms the alternative questions:

> Are the teachers of the school content to belong, as individuals, to the School of Spiritual Science in Dornach or do they want to join with the character 'as teacher of the Free Waldorf School'? Then the teachers would make it necessary that the Pedagogical Section in Dornach concerns itself with the Free Waldorf School, while it would otherwise focus only on pedagogy in general. Thus, it really is a great difference.[132]

Which of the two options Rudolf Steiner favoured (and spiritually *must* favour) was clear. When Lilly Kolisko asked him shortly afterwards if she could take shorthand notes of the Class Lessons in order to present them to Stuttgart anthroposophists, he allowed her to do it, with the wish, however, that she would not present them to just any group of anthroposophists, but directly to the *teacher faculty* of the Waldorf School, with whom he could and wanted to work esoterically. ('Then Dr Steiner continued: "Would you not like to convey this to the Teacher Faculty of the Waldorf School?" Of course, I was prepared to do this and Dr Steiner promised to issue the necessary membership cards for the *entire faculty* immediately.'[133]) Therefore, it can be assumed that the Stuttgart faculty adopted as their own direction what Rudolf Steiner recommended and founded on 5 February 1924. It was sensible and correct—the Dornach School of Spiritual Science wanted and had to be active and productive in the professional areas, to which pedagogy belonged. Membership in the Dornach School of Spiritual Science was not only a matter of a personal training-path—with which members of the Anthroposophical Society and co-workers of the Stuttgart School were already indirectly involved—but further signified the prerequisite for the Christmas Conference impulse to take effect within the Waldorf School. The teacher faculty could become an esoteric organ. ('*The faculty should form a core, from which something can radiate.*'[134]) In this sense, Lilly Kolisko also held the First Class Lessons for the community of teachers.[135] The Free Waldorf School's public education conference, 'The Position of Education in the Personal and Cultural Life of the Present' (7 to 13 April 1924), was arranged in Stuttgart by 'The Executive Council of the General Anthroposophical Society' and 'The Teacher Faculty of the Free Waldorf

School' working *together* for the first time, as responsible organizers.[136] Rudolf Steiner presented the programme and the goals of the conference, which he single-handedly formulated, to all colleagues of his 'esoteric Council' in Dornach for agreement ('for written agreement by the current Executive Council') and signed it himself, followed first by Albert Steffen, Ita Wegman, Marie Steiner, Günther Wachsmuth and Elisabeth Vreede.[137] Thus, a new epoch began for the Waldorf School and teacher faculty, working together and belonging to the Dornach School of Spiritual Science.

*

The situation within the medical profession should be considered differently, for this group was not a community; it was exceptionally diversified in its activity, and anything but homogenous—in clinics and practices with their various tasks, prerequisites and goals. Many doctors probably made the 'connection to Dornach' as a personal decision. Of special interest for understanding the situation after the Christmas Conference and for Rudolf Steiner's intentions are the activities within the group of 'young doctors'. This was an initially loose association of medical students and young doctors, who first met with Rudolf Steiner in autumn 1922—dissatisfied with the bourgeois tendencies of the anthroposophical medical profession, ensouled with the spirit of a new beginning and seeking a real 'humanization' of medicine.[138] In January and April 1924, these medical students and doctors received special courses of instruction from Rudolf Steiner—which were de facto the first courses stemming from the School of Spiritual Science after the Christmas Conference—followed a path of esoteric-mantric development and were committed to the spirit of the Class Lessons through their specific professional field.[139] Although members of the audience were for the most part unusually young, did not all belong to the Anthroposophical Society and in no way thought about applying for membership in the Dornach School of Spiritual Science, Rudolf Steiner received the 'young doctors' as a closed group or circle, and did this *out of his own initiative* before the beginning of the Easter course in the School of Spiritual Science. Madeleine van Deventer wrote: 'It seems important for me to mention that right after arriving in Dornach, we received our certificates as members of the First Class of the School of Spiritual Science; even those who had submitted no application received them.'[140] It is further documented that Rudolf Steiner's newsletter to the 'young doctors' group dated 11 March 1924, was designated by him in the Class Lesson of Good Friday, 18 April, as a communication to Class members '*from out of the work of the School of Spiritual Science*', although at the time of writing the newsletter he had not yet accepted them (rather he had done this only shortly before the Class Lesson). 'The members of the School of Spiritual Science should in the future hear, through such newsletters, about the continuation of the School's work in specific professional fields',[141] about 'what flows through this School in Dornach'.[142] Rudolf Steiner started this with his medical 'newsletter' of 11 March 1924—in answer to questions he received from the group of listeners at the January course, and whom he admitted by signing their certificates together with Ita Wegman. The newsletter began with the text:

> In accord with a promise we once made at the Christmas Conference, we are sending in this first newsletter our communications about the guidance of the Medical Section at the Goetheanum, to those connected with us in the cultivation of medicine. It is issued with the conviction that we are united in the New Year through the medical courses.[143]

Rudolf Steiner and Ita Wegman spoke about the already-existing connection—created by the course and in-itself esoteric—between the School of Spiritual Science and its Medical Section ('for those *connected with us* in the cultivation of medicine'). The January and April 1924 courses belonged not only to the first esoteric and exoteric training and education activities for the Medical Section at the Goetheanum, but also to the formative process of this Section itself—as the Medical Section of the new School of Spiritual Science. Course attendants should not only listen to and personally process the lectures, but should be active as a community in the sense of the Dornach impulse. Rudolf Steiner spoke about an 'alliance' of the group as a 'link to Dornach'—a connection '*by you with us here*'—and spoke directly in the January course of the fundamental situation: that is, the new beginning of the Anthroposophical Movement after the Christmas Conference:

> From now on there must be a sort of upswing in the entire conception of the Anthroposophical Movement and of the individual areas. While you are initially seeking your medical path, you must also inwardly participate from the beginning on in this real upswing in such a way that you are not, so to say, just making a contribution

on the esoteric path—but that it must be a matter of fully imbuing your way of life with esoteric impulses.[144]

With this as a background, which contains a real understanding of the Sections of the School of Spiritual Science as concrete research- and training-centre, the connection to Dornach was both meaningful and important for all of the 'young doctors'. Rudolf Steiner attributed the initiation-level spiritual work that he accomplished in Dornach for the individual Sections to the esoteric School itself—to which the responsible cooperating professional circles naturally had to belong. Rudolf Steiner's research in specific areas and the collaboration he initiated with the respective Section leaders stood, as research- and teaching-activity, in the centre of the spiritual tasks of the Sections. From this centre, spiritual-scientific assistance should be given to each professional area: specific initiation knowledge, research methods and tasks, which should benefit the professional members connected with the School of Spiritual Science—and through them the world:

> In this sense, my dear friends, we want to remain united—we want to remain so united that you will keep the Goetheanum here in Dornach as your centre-point and really support this centre-point, so that this centre-point can work into the world through you.[145]

Out of the young doctors' circle—as a medical Class-community—there was finally also formed the 'esoteric core of the Medical Section', with which Rudolf Steiner wanted to begin a new medical Mystery-training and unfold the Medical Section further—though this did not happen, due to his illness and finally his death.[146]

★

Recollecting the relationship of the Christian Community priests to the Dornach School of Spiritual Science and the final Apocalypse Course heard in Dornach in September 1924, Gottfried Husemann wrote in a reflective essay: '"*I will accept you all into the First Class of the School of Spiritual Science*", he [Rudolf Steiner] said directly in the welcoming speech. This happened then in the following days and thus priests, besides those attending the Apocalypse lectures and evening lessons [the karma lectures], could also participate in the first course of the Michael School. "You will also", he added "receive the letters of the School". With respect to these letters nothing further came about. "The relationship to the Anthroposophical Movement will become ever more intimate".'[147] Like the teachers of the Stuttgart Waldorf School, some Christian Community priests had already spoken with Rudolf Steiner in February 1924 about the future relationship of the Christian Community to the General Anthroposophical Society and its newly founded Dornach School of Spiritual Science.[148] At this time, Rudolf Steiner had already affirmed the intended intensification of cooperative work, also at the level of the First Class, as well as his intention to write letters for members of the School of Spiritual Science—with which he (together with Ita Wegman) made an initial start in March. He did not strive for a theological Section in Dornach; instead he pleaded for a continuation of the Christian Community work developed in Stuttgart since autumn 1922, in research, teaching, and cultic practice. Rudolf Steiner energetically supported an active participation of the priests, individually and as an esoteric community, in the Dornach developments already begun. He made possible in September 1924—as in the case of the 'young doctors' one-half year earlier, however now at the request of Friedrich Rittelmeyer—membership in the School of Spiritual Science, even for those priests who had not been in the Anthroposophical Society for two years, and those who didn't even belong to it at all. The Christian Community and its supporting personalities were undoubtedly very important to Rudolf Steiner; in a conference in June 1924 he said in Stuttgart to Waldorf teachers: 'You must always remember: Christian Community priests belong to [...] the anthroposophists who have in the shortest time made the greatest progress. The priests are not the same as they were; they have achieved tremendous inner development. The priests have achieved exemplary development in their entire soul-life in the short time since the endeavour began. Not all, of course; but by and large, and in all areas, they work beneficially.'[149] In the Apocalypse Course, Rudolf Steiner finally spoke about 'what the Christian Community can do to become the bearer of an essential part of the New Mysteries'[150] and thereby indirectly about their affiliation with the tasks of the Dornach School of Spiritual Science, about which he said elsewhere: 'The Mysteries themselves have receded in the time during which free human development had to secure a place. Now the time has come when the Mysteries must again be found. They must be found again. One should be fully conscious of this, that today arrangements must be made to find the Mysteries again. Out of this consciousness the Christmas Conference was held, for it is an urgent necessity that there be on Earth a place where the Mysteries can once again be founded. In its further development, the Anthroposophical Society must become the path to the renewed Mysteries.'[151]

Even when many of the questions connected with these procedures are still not sufficiently answered, the historical consideration shows at least what significance Rudolf Steiner placed on the inner connection to the School of Spiritual Science, not only for individuals but also for communities of people—for communities whose specific professional tasks are insolubly connected with the effectiveness of the Dornach School of Spiritual Science in civilization. That 'which is really wanted today from the Goetheanum for world- and civilizational-development',[152] can only be brought into the world by people—esoterically connected with one another—who stand for Dornach and its spirituality and are prepared to represent this specific spirituality in the world's various areas of activity: 'I am here as representative of the anthroposophy issuing from the Goetheanum.'[153]

In summer 1924 Rudolf Steiner wrote in the internal newsletter of the General Anthroposophical Society ('*What is Happening in the Anthroposophical Society*'):

> There is a difference between the sectarian advocacy of something which one has worked out as dogmatic anthroposophy, and the upright, open, unconcealed, and unembellished advocacy of what comes to light through anthroposophy regarding knowledge of the spiritual world, so that the human being can gain a humanly worthy relationship to this world. [...] There can only be the judgement: '*Anthroposophy is there, it has been developed; I join with it so that what has been developed will become known in the world.*'[154]

Part II

Sergei O. Prokofieff

HOW DO WE STAND BEFORE RUDOLF STEINER TODAY?

'How do we stand *before* Rudolf Steiner?'
Peter Selg[155]

Preface

> 'And when you see the hideous forms
> which arise when the true self of Man errs—
> the prophet Daniel says that they will arise
> in the Holy Place [...] you should know that
> it is near, before the very doors.'
> *Matthew 24:15 and 33 (J. Madsen Tr.)*

My address on 30 March 2012, the anniversary of Rudolf Steiner's death, which I held in painful dismay and out of inner obligation, has been discussed actively in broad circles of the Anthroposophical Society. In the process, questions have been raised, the answers to which I think are important for the future of the Goetheanum and the Society.

The basis for these discussions—in addition to the lecture itself, which, due to its relation to the Annual General Meeting of the General Anthroposophical Society, was attended by about 700 people—was the publication of a short summary kindly composed by a member of the audience, Gerlinde Schultz from Friedrichsdorf. This summary was published in a new, electronically distributed newsletter, founded by Roland Tüscher and Kirsten Juel after the elimination of the [members'] insert in the weekly magazine [*Das Goetheanum*], as its continuation as a member-initiative. (The summary appeared specifically in *Initiative Entwicklungsrichtung Anthroposophie* No. 8, dated 8 April 2012.) Thus, the essential content of my lecture could be made known also to a larger circle of people.

Because the problems within the Anthroposophical Society and above all at the Goetheanum—touched on in my lecture—have provoked a lively and engaged interest on the part of members, I have decided to publish the full text here with some clarifying remarks and supplementary comments as added notes.[156]

The publishing of the full text seems to me all the more important because it is possible that a lack of awareness of its precise wording has led to strongly divergent opinions about my contribution. Along with enthusiastic and positive reports—that finally a certain unspoken taboo has been broken, and with this, communication opened regarding the burning question of the connection of the Society and the Goetheanum to anthroposophy and to Rudolf Steiner—there were, on the other hand, also keenly disapproving attitudes. However, I am pleased that the positive reactions have by far predominated, and I am grateful for the many letters of thanks and encouragement that I have received lately, as they show that love for Rudolf Steiner and uncompromising support for anthroposophy continue to live as active impulses in many members. It is these forces alone that can ensure the future of our Society and of anthroposophy in the world, in the sense that Rudolf Steiner intended.

At the end of my lecture, I spoke about a certain photograph of Rudolf Steiner that now stands beside the lectern on the stage of the Great Hall, since I succeeded in having it brought there from its prior banishment to the Goetheanum's back staircase.[157] With this gesture, due respect is shown to the founder of anthroposophy and to the Goetheanum. For one can only consider it a shocking symptom of an increasing process of deterioration at the Goetheanum that, in recent years, little by little, all photographs of Rudolf Steiner have been removed from the public rooms of the building he constructed—so that on the occasion of his 150th birthday, a single picture of Rudolf Steiner appeared in the back staircase, fastened to the rough cement wall and surrounded by empty picture-frames. In addition to this is the fact that it was located in a place which, approximately 84 years after the building was opened, has still not been completed—and of all possible occasions, on the 150th anniversary of Rudolf Steiner's birth was used as a new exhibition room.[158]

Such treatment of a significant person—in this case Rudolf Steiner, to whom those teaching and active at the Goetheanum have everything to be thankful for—I have never encountered at any time in my many travels throughout the world. And I have been able to visit many such historic places: the Goethe House, Schiller House, Lessing House, Albrecht Dürer's house, Ralph Waldo Emerson's house, the residence of Dostoyevsky, the country estates of Tolstoy and George Washington, and many others. Everywhere, in rich and poor circumstances, I have always encountered reverent love and deep regard for these great people, which have been visible in the minutest details, and comprise the special atmosphere and appeal of the places in which they once lived and worked. In contrast to this, nowhere have I met the kind of indifference and disrespect towards the person who once lived and was active in such a place as, I am greatly saddened to say, has been the case here at the Goetheanum in recent years.

It is not at all a matter of making icons out of Rudolf Steiner's photographs. However, one should feel obligated to maintain at least the *very most basic* standards of decency and respect that one finds everywhere else in the world in the culture of significant places. In other words: shocking signs, showing a lack of civility, reveal that the Goetheanum falls far below the commonly accepted standard for such significant places of culture.

In this regard, one must unfortunately conclude with great pain that the Goetheanum has for a long time lagged behind what, generally in the world, is regarded as an expression of appreciation and respect. Just one small example of this: Can you imagine entering the Goethe or Schiller House and not being able to learn at all to whom it once belonged, who built it, lived, and was active there? No one who truly loves Goethe or Schiller can really imagine that—and it is also in fact not the case in Weimar, where they lived. Yet this is precisely the situation with regard to Rudolf Steiner and the Goetheanum—the place of his most important activity—which every visitor has been encountering in an increasingly apparent way now for years. As a pupil of Rudolf Steiner, one can only be deeply ashamed and outraged at this.

A further unpleasant question must be raised in this Preface. In discussions about my lecture, uneasiness was also expressed that my critical remarks regarding the grievances in the Anthroposophical Society and in the Goetheanum were spoken in connection with the anniversary of Rudolf Steiner's death. That this was indeed called for, I stood and still stand—even in retrospect—in full and complete assurance. And this is due to the following reasons: The grievances to which I referred, and whose number could even be extended, are of the same kind as those causes which, among others at that time, led to Rudolf Steiner's having to leave the physical plane prematurely—and as a consequence of which he was unable to complete his work on Earth. The catastrophic results of this fact are painfully known to every anthroposophist concerned with what Rudolf Steiner intended with the Christmas Conference, the new foundation of the Society, the karma lectures, and the School of Spiritual Science.

Rudolf Steiner himself pointed out—one can almost sense, as if in a moment of despair—that he felt treated by the members as a 'negligible quantity'.[159] He also expressed this in other places, especially when he spoke about the 'inner opposition' against him on the part of members of the Anthroposophical Society.[160] For once we must really allow ourselves to look plainly at this: pupils who are opposed to their spiritual teacher!

And this was one of the reasons that it was impossible for Rudolf Steiner to continue working on Earth in the 20th century. Further still, one must observe today with alarm that this opposition to Rudolf Steiner has increased considerably in our circles. The facts mentioned in my lecture are only one small indication of that reality. Therefore, such observations also belong to the anniversary of Rudolf Steiner's death. I sincerely hope that with my remarks I can reach the hearts of some anthroposophists of our time, for these are words that should contribute to reflection and awakening.

Finally, I want to note that to me it is not a matter of quickly taking a few 'cosmetic measures' and immediately mounting a photo of Rudolf Steiner, along with facts about his life, near the West entrance.[161] Rather, the intention of my lecture was, and continues to be, to draw attention to the fact that the recent development of the Goetheanum is no longer heading in the right direction; rather, it is heading in a direction that can be considered neither in the spirit intended by Rudolf Steiner, nor of service to anthroposophy. Before it is too late, this direction must be altered very decisively and with full force. Otherwise, the Goetheanum is in danger—if I may use Peter Selg's expression here—of being degraded to spiritual 'insignificance', and of becoming a mere combination of museum and conference-centre. In this regard, Peter Selg writes: 'If this effort fails, then the Society prepared by Rudolf Steiner will without doubt die, gradually or abruptly, in the coming years and decades; and the Goetheanum as such, despite its exceedingly important Section-work and social relationships, will become spiritually and substantively insignificant. With this, however, something essential would be lost for many centuries.'[162]

So that this does not happen, and in order for the necessary changes to be made, a fundamental 'temple cleansing' must be undertaken. 'But', as Marie Steiner stated in 1948, 'such a healing is only possible if we return to Dr Steiner's guidelines'.[163]

It is to be hoped that my lecture on the anniversary of Rudolf Steiner's death will be a contribution towards the first step being taken in the Anthroposophical Society, and above all at the Goetheanum, in a new direction in accord with the spirit of Rudolf Steiner.

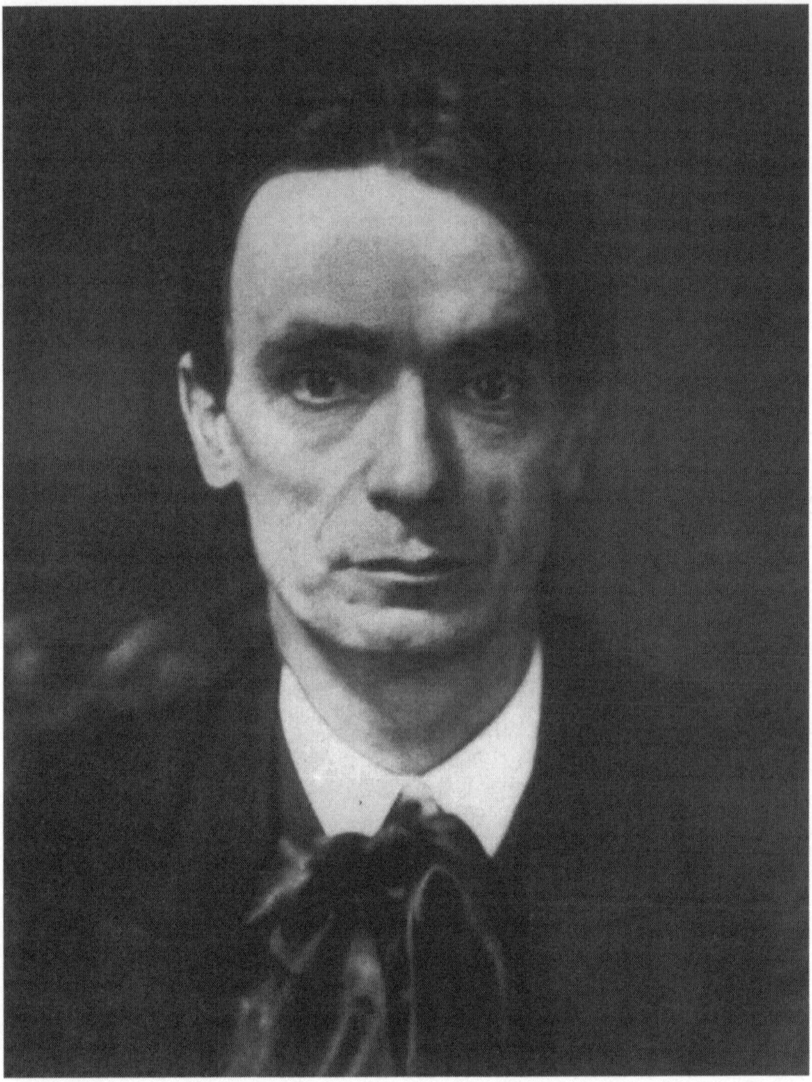

On the Anniversary of Rudolf Steiner's Death

Lecture of 30 March 2012

> 'You see him [his stature] as much too small.'
> Ita Wegman[164]

Dear members of the Anthroposophical Society, dear friends,

Today we think about many members of this Society from all over the world, some of them our close friends, who have crossed the threshold to the spiritual world since the last Annual General Meeting here at the Goetheanum. Above all, however, we think about the 87th anniversary of Rudolf Steiner's death. When we really think about our Society spiritually, we should never forget that it has nearly as many members in the spiritual world as here on Earth. For there are a large number, among them also significant individualities, who in the past one hundred years have crossed the threshold to the spiritual world in unbreakable loyalty to this Society, to anthroposophy, and especially to Rudolf Steiner.

At the beginning of this lecture, I would like to mention three people who have returned to their spiritual home since the last Annual General Meeting. I was connected with the first personality as colleague in the Executive Council, and enjoyed working with him for many years. That was Heinz Zimmermann (1937 to 2011), whom many people in this auditorium also knew well. I would like to characterize briefly two special attributes of this human soul. Heinz Zimmermann was from the outset a talented Waldorf teacher. In addition to this capability, something even more significant developed in his biography. As well as this very notable talent as teacher, he had a special social competence. This could be experienced by everyone who had the pleasure of working with Heinz Zimmermann.

In the present period of 'I'-development, where everything social is difficult to develop, real social competence can be seen, among other things, when a person is able to keep in balance what he feels as an obligation to pure truth on the one hand, and the impulse for brotherhood on the other. It may be the most difficult thing in social life to keep these polarities joined together in harmony. Thinking of Heinz

Zimmermann, I want to say that he was a real master in this complicated area. One could learn from him, as I experienced in the years I worked with him on the Executive Council and in the faculty of the School of Spiritual Science, much of importance for the present and future.

Along with this, he had a second special characteristic. For decades, Heinz Zimmermann was especially connected with what one can call the singular language of Rudolf Steiner. Rarely have I met a native German speaker who had such a fine, differentiated and deep connection to Rudolf Steiner's language and could speak so wonderfully, edifyingly and movingly about it, fully convinced that Rudolf Steiner's language is in no way outmoded (as is often expressed in our circles) or perhaps only had validity at the beginning of the 20th century—but that it is a true Mystery-language, meaning not a language from the past, but one that comes to us from out of the future.

One must understand that if the German language is to have a future, despite the signs of degradation visible everywhere in Central Europe, its only salvation lies in the possibility that Rudolf Steiner's language will penetrate it with the impulse of Michael, the present-day Time Spirit. This is one of Heinz Zimmermann's great intentions. He carried the message of this singular, thoroughly modern language of Rudolf Steiner, which at the same time is the language of the New Mysteries, to all places he visited and travelled to. In particular, he tried to convince those native German speakers. When I express it in this way, it may appear as a paradox to some people, but it is so.

The second personality whom I would like to mention here lives, in an archetypical way for our time, between the stars and the Earth with her very special talent for connecting the heavenly processes with those of the Earth, particularly in the area of plants. I am speaking about Maria Thun (1922 to 2012), who has very recently crossed over the threshold to the spiritual world. One of the great achievements in her life—known worldwide and also surely by many people present here—is the *Sowing Calendar* by Maria Thun, called the *Aussaattage*, which is concerned with the connection between heaven and Earth and very delicately shows the first beginnings of what will reach its full effectiveness sometime in the distant future: namely that the Earth will no longer live and weave in separation from the sun, but will once again be united with the sun.

Thus, we can have the feeling that something lived in Maria Thun which Goethe expressed archetypically in the figure of Makarie from his novel *Wilhelm Meister's Journeyman Years*—who now no longer lives in devotion to the course of the stars alone, with the course of the planets, but, as a new Makarie in Maria Thun, connects herself with anthroposophy and the Goetheanum and then turns her gaze downward from the stars to Mother Earth in order to unite them with one another.

Proceeding from this, the *Aussaattage* was used in many countries of the Earth: from Russia to America; from Central Europe to South American countries and Australia. Even though in our circles some scepticism was levied against Maria Thun's work, in practical life numerous experiences in the most diverse places of the Earth have proved what her *Aussaattage* portrayed from year to year to be fruitful. For it is significant on which day seeds are sown, on what day harvest occurs and on what day and how the various plants are cultivated. Maria Thun's message about the relationship of the stars to the plant world of the Earth is quite real and practical. Herein lies something of the future as well!

The third personality I will mention here is Erdmuth Grosse (1928 to 2012). Although he was increasingly bed-ridden due to a difficult illness, he worked with determination on a theme that concerned him for years and decades: the different karmic streams connected with the individuals Rudolf Steiner called into the founding Executive Council at the Christmas Conference. Erdmuth Grosse wrote his last book about these five outstanding people, who after Rudolf Steiner's death developed such difficulties with one another that our Society had to relive these for decades as a sort of karmic necessity. In it he showed that this trial which the Anthroposophical Society had to undergo should lead not to death, but to a continual spiritual awakening and in the end, to a renewed union of all involved. We should never forget that this unification could still be accomplished after the two great ruptures in our Society.

Thus, in the last years of his life Erdmuth Grosse undertook the difficult task, in his book, to characterize all five members of the founding Executive Council with their karmic backgrounds. What's more, this rather extensive book was sold out right after its publication. This shows that even today, although for a long time no member of the founding Executive Council has been living on Earth, the question of the riddle, the secret of this Executive Council in our Society, is still very alive.

If one becomes absorbed with the content of this book—not necessarily needing to agree with all of the author's thoughts—he can be deeply moved by the gesture of reconciliation proceeding from it. There is not the slightest indication of a judgement, no condemnation or criticism; rather only and alone this wonderful archetypal Christian gesture with a view directed to the beauty and greatness that lived in these five personalities without exception, and continues to live even stronger today in the spiritual world. These five members of the founding Executive Council were brought closer to the reader in this special atmosphere of reconciliation, of brotherhood; in the foreground stood above all their dedicated loyalty to anthroposophy and to Rudolf Steiner, which these five individuals, whether when together or later separated from one another, carried within themselves until the last breath of their lives—in order, after crossing the threshold, to work together with Rudolf Steiner once again in the spiritual world. Thus, after reading this book one feels strongly convinced that these five personalities—Marie Steiner, Ita Wegman, Albert Steffen, Elisabeth Vreede and Günther Wachsmuth—continue to be inseparably connected with Rudolf Steiner in the deepest sense, and in a manner exemplary for us all.

★

However, today we are thinking primarily about the anniversary of Rudolf Steiner's death. If we look at the last years of his life, we see the Christmas Conference of 1923/24 like an illuminated peak, like the culmination of his complete biography. This deed of Rudolf Steiner's was so new and future-oriented that he referred, on two occasions, to the previous development of anthroposophy on Earth through nearly three seven-year periods as a preparation for what could occur at the Christmas Conference: namely the possibility to speak directly from the archetypal source of anthroposophical esotericism.[165]

We all know well how this Christmas Conference came about. However, we can gain still greater understanding when we know that it occurred in the wake of the Anthroposophical Society's deepest crisis: that is, following the burning of the first Goetheanum, which was brought about by the bitterest enemies of anthroposophy. This work of Rudolf Steiner's now lay in ruins. What sorrow and pain Rudolf Steiner experienced from this tragedy during the night of the fire, in which ten years of his work, something that was to become a visible symbol of anthroposophy on Earth, was taken away from humanity—this, none of us can truly comprehend. This time the fire was caused not, as in the case of the temple at Ephesus, through the envy of the gods; rather it was the envy and hatred of human beings that destroyed this special building.[166]

Then in the course of 1923, something occurred that was so truly unique that we cannot grasp its magnificence without further preparation.

This pain, this sorrow, was transformed in Rudolf Steiner's soul into pure love, quite in the sense of true Manichaeism. For all the hatred and antipathy, all the turmoil and confusion surrounding the burned Goetheanum was not simply dismissed by Rudolf Steiner; rather he received it into his soul and transformed it in the sense of the true Manichean impulse,[167] in pure love, from which he created the Foundation Stone of Love during the Christmas Conference as the cornerstone for a new human community, a new Anthroposophical Society.

If we seek a model or archetype for this deed of Rudolf Steiner's, then we should look to the events of the Turning Point of Time, where out of the unimaginable pain of a god on Earth, on the Golgotha hill, the spirit of all-embracing love was born here on Earth at Whitsun.[168] In this metamorphosis—in the transformation of the suffering on Golgotha in the stream of the spirit, in the stream of all-embracing spiritual love, which radiated into the souls of human beings on Whitsun morning—we may see the archetype of what has now been accomplished on the human level, in real terms and in the midst of humanity, by Rudolf Steiner between the burning of the Goetheanum and the Christmas Conference.

Now there is an important statement that Rudolf Steiner made about the Christmas Conference, which he expressed on 6 February 1924; he was staying in Stuttgart during the initial period after the Christmas Conference, which at that time was the largest anthroposophical community. Rudolf Steiner reported there about the Christmas Conference and uttered the important statement, which one should always contemplate in his own meditation as the true test of his own conscience. This statement is: 'Thus it comes to this: that with regard to the anthroposophical cause, this Christmas Conference is either nothing or everything.'[169]

If we follow Rudolf Steiner's life further, then out of the course of his life we will be able to convince ourselves that the decision for the Christmas Conference was actually quite radical for him: nothing or everything! Out of what he accomplished after the Christmas Conference, we can gather with certainty that it was and remained everything for him.

Above all, three initiatives proceeded from this impulse: the building of the second Goetheanum—of which he could leave us only the external model—the karma lectures and the founding of the Michael School on Earth.

In order to understand the second building, one needs only to compare the first Goetheanum, based on its model, with the second. Then one will quickly realize what the Mystery of the transition from the first to the second building consists of. The first Goetheanum was entirely oriented from centre to periphery. Once while on his way there, Rudolf Steiner stated that he would have preferred to have constructed this building completely under the Earth, with only an inner form and without any external shape. The formative impulse came directly from the centre, out of the 'I' of humanity. Through the tragic fire on New Year's Eve 1922/1923, this Goetheanum was taken away from us all. It ascended into heaven, and the earthly affair became a cosmic affair.[170] Then, in the expanses of the ether-cosmos was born the 'good spirit of the Goetheanum',[171] which Rudolf Steiner was now able to receive as cosmic spirit, and whose being he then imprinted into earthly substance.

Consisting of plasticine, the model of the second Goetheanum had, however, no interior space; in this way one senses that all of its formative forces came from outside, from the periphery of the world. One imagines how Rudolf Steiner modelled hour after hour, and how from out of this movement from outside to inside, solid material was penetrated with this spirit of the Goetheanum which had become cosmic.

Now we can ask ourselves: What actually happens when the interior becomes exterior, and when thereby something from the periphery works upon us? From where do we know this experience? Every one of us knows it, because we have each already gone through the gate of death many times in our previous incarnations. Both in death, as well as by correctly crossing the threshold on the path to initiation, it comes to pass that what we previously carried within us as our soul-world becomes our spiritual environment: We are surrounded from outside with this new cosmic reality. The interior becomes exterior in the spiritual sense and illuminates us from the periphery of the world. That is the secret of the threshold! This secret lies, along with many others, behind the transition from the first to the second building. This touches upon and artistically portrays the fact that in our time, all of humanity has unconsciously crossed over the threshold to the spiritual world.[172]

Then there are the karma lectures. How can we even approximately understand this powerful cycle of 82 lectures? How can its background be discovered? Rudolf Steiner already gave a clue for this much earlier. In 1911 he said that we live in a time during which Christ will increasingly become Lord of Karma.[173] It is Christ himself who, for the well-being of humanity, unites the various karmic threads into a new, future-oriented sun fabric.

If we want to become conscious co-workers of Christ in the field of karma in our time or in the future, then we should know—that is, we must learn—how karma works; how it is formed in individual human destinies, as well as the destiny of groups of people and in the entire history of mankind. With the karma lectures, Rudolf Steiner gave us a guide so that we may prepare ourselves in this or a future earthly life to become conscious co-workers of Christ in the new formation of karma.

The third event that came as a result of the Christmas Conference was the founding of the Michael School on the Earth.[174] As many of you know, Rudolf Steiner continually emphasized that he was not the founder of this School, but only the mediator for Michael—as the leading spirit of our epoch—to establish his School on Earth. He, the Time Spirit, is the true founder and director of this School.

How did it come to pass that Michael could accomplish his first deed on Earth in this way? This was only possible through Rudolf Steiner's sacrificial deed at the Christmas Conference—through that which was here carried to the spiritual world, as new creation, by a human being out of his complete freedom. This is precisely the Foundation Stone of Love, which was created by Rudolf Steiner during the Christmas Conference from the highest forces of the Trinity itself,[175] in order to bring it as offering to Michael in the spiritual world.[176]

On other occasions, especially in the lectures on Rudolf Steiner's biography, I have spoken more extensively about this.[177] In answer to this creative deed of Rudolf Steiner's, to this new creation, there now follows—because Michael is an active and creative spirit—a *hierarchical deed*. Michael answered this free human deed by founding his School on Earth: an event for which there is no parallel in all human history.

This was the third foundation by Rudolf Steiner from out of the esoteric impulse of the Christmas Conference. He created for Michael the possibility to work here on Earth for the future development of humanity in an entirely different way than he otherwise could. From this we can discern the dimension of our responsibility in relation to the founding of the Michael School on Earth, as expression of the greatest trust of the Time Spirit towards his pupils. And they must prove themselves worthy of this trust by remaining loyal in their hearts towards this gift, protecting and further cultivating it. This and much else make it possible for us to have a sense of Rudolf Steiner's greatness, which was made apparent above all in the time after the Christmas Conference.

At the present time, and this is also the case in anthroposophical circles, a serious problem is evident. I have reflected much about how this has actually come to be: that there are always anthroposophists who for years spend their time either seeking alleged mistakes by Rudolf Steiner, or entering into endless discussions as to whether something racist can be found in Rudolf Steiner's formulations—whereby for someone who really knows this work, it should be obvious there is and can be absolutely nothing racist with Rudolf Steiner. What gives rise to this strange endeavour: to want to find something in relation to Rudolf Steiner that is totally foreign to him, and that under no circumstances belongs to this high individual? Where does this pursuit come from—this mixture of love and hatred on the part of some of his students towards their teacher? So far, I have only been able to find one answer.

With the inner approach to Rudolf Steiner—which is unavoidable during serious occupation with his work—such people simply cannot stand his greatness. That is, if a person tries to approach Rudolf Steiner spiritually, this path becomes very dramatic. It is like the path to one's own higher 'I', to one's own higher being, and inevitably leads one close to the threshold. However, here stands the severe guardian, who simply shows to a person in an unvarnished way that despite everything he has become accustomed to believe about his own importance, there is in reality very little and perhaps even less than little.

If a person, however, has the courage to compare his deeds and achievements in life with those of Rudolf Steiner and to withstand this discrepancy, then he stands as though before his higher 'I'.[178] If on the training-path one has certain spiritual experiences—be they ever so slight—and tries during the search for Rudolf Steiner in the spiritual world to come into connection with him, then he will discover that on the one hand he comes much closer to Rudolf Steiner as personal spiritual teacher, but on the other hand he perceives with terror how far he is from his own higher being, which one experiences with Rudolf Steiner in full splendour, in full brilliance. In certain circumstances this cannot be endured.

This means however, that when a person has not completed this trial and doesn't notice that the problem lies alone in himself rather than with Rudolf Steiner, then it can happen that this person wants to degrade Rudolf Steiner to his own, much lower level, in order that he can stand to a certain extent next to Rudolf Steiner and content himself with what he experiences as his shattering nothingness when attempting to approach Rudolf Steiner in the spirit. For many of Rudolf Steiner's students this is a true threshold-situation of the present time, even though it often does not work its way into consciousness.

There is something else as well. Already in earlier years there was much discussion about whether or not one should revere Rudolf Steiner. Naturally, in our consciousness soul period the formulation 'whether one should do something or not' is totally inappropriate, because everyone must decide that for himself. However, it is frequently overlooked that there are two different kinds of reverence. The first takes place on a quite naïve level in a small child. As parents and teachers, we know how important it is for this naïve reverence in children to be cultivated and developed, so that later they will be capable of becoming earnest students of the spirit. Rudolf Steiner speaks about this in his book *Knowledge of the Higher Worlds: How is it Achieved?*[179]

It is lamentable, however, when a person remains such a naïve admirer in mature years! Following this, the nature of the person himself comes to expression. For in the period of transition into adolescence, we experience impulses of inner defiance towards all authority and often even become true rebels. We want to explore, test and conquer everything with our own awakened thinking. At this age we even feel ourselves to be almost on equal footing with the great thinkers of all times. This doesn't, however, have anything to do with the inner maturity of the human being's soul. For that comes to be established only much later. Thinking, however, is first made equally available to all people [as is experienced in this stage].

Therefore, it is natural and fully justified when at times young people express criticism towards Rudolf Steiner and distance themselves from him. For that belongs to this particular age. This is completely understandable and should in no way be judged negatively. When, for example, children from anthroposophical families go out into the world and don't want to hear anything about anthroposophy and Rudolf Steiner for years, this is quite understandable. But it is regrettable when, later on as a mature person, one remains stuck in a state of adolescence or once again reverts back to the child-like condition of admiration. For at this point something has changed fundamentally. The person must now realize that the admiration of a human being, a person, is no longer appropriate; rather it is a matter of the path of inner development and the reverence towards truth and knowledge. From now on, this becomes a new guiding principle for him. Then he can no longer revere a person as long as that person's being is not aligned with the truth, which is indeed the case with most people today.

By turning, in a great leap, to the highest archetype in this connection, we find at the Turning Point of Time the conversation between Pilate and Christ Jesus, in which Pilate poses the question: 'What is truth?' (John 18:38)—the question of a clever, educated Roman. To his surprise, he doesn't receive an answer. Why does his interlocutor remain silent? Because the being who stands before Pilate was and is the only one on the Earth who could accurately say: '*I am the truth*' (John 14:16). This means Pilate posed his question in a fundamentally wrong way. He actually should have asked Christ Jesus: '*Who* is the truth?' Then would have followed the only correct answer: '*I am!*' And Pilate could have become a pupil of Christ Jesus.[180] Thus, one can say: In Christ Jesus there came to expression the only concrete personality, living on the Earth, filled with World-Truth.

If a person tries to think about *this*, he will soon notice how difficult it is to grasp these thoughts at all. Nevertheless, one actually contains within oneself the archetype of Christian initiation as such. Precisely all of the great Christian Initiates were drawn towards this from the beginning. For our time it was Rudolf Steiner!

This means that when a person approaches the anthroposophical training-path as the modern form of Christian initiation, not abstractly but quite concretely, then this path is such that the Initiate gradually unites his personality, living and active on Earth, more and more with the Being of Truth. In this way, he gradually becomes truth himself, a representative of the truth of the spiritual world, as Rudolf Steiner expressed in thousands of lectures resulting from his spiritual research.

Could one sincerely claim that someone able to research in the spiritual world in *such* a way as Rudolf Steiner did, could carry truth within himself as an earthly personality without being deeply affected by this truth? This cannot be conceived in the sense of the archetype of Christian initiation. If one has once discovered the truth with regard to Rudolf Steiner in this way—however, not abstractly, but by saying: 'Rudolf Steiner stands before me as a concrete earthly personality, and here is the truth he proclaimed'—then, whilst searching for Rudolf Steiner in the spiritual world, one experiences how the truth and the personality of this man gradually begin to flow together in the light of the archetype of Christ Jesus. Then the reverence towards truth can no longer be separated from the reverence for the person who lived the truth on Earth. This is no longer naïve admiration, but a new, mature reverence that has been achieved on a long path to knowledge.

Moreover, a person then knows from his own experience that he cannot find Rudolf Steiner in the spiritual world in any other way than through recognizing: In him, the truth of the higher worlds which he proclaimed throughout his life cannot be separated from his person. That is also the deeper meaning of his statement that one may not separate his work from his name.[181] For in his person, also during his earthly life, this was to be seen esoterically as a unity.

When one realizes this, one will also come to clarity about what Rudolf Steiner—as the leading representative of the consciousness soul,[182] who proclaimed the truth of the spiritual world in countless lectures and books—signifies for our time. For the true spiritual world is precisely the world of pure truth. Rudolf Steiner could speak of this spiritual world throughout the almost unimaginable scope of around 350 volumes of his complete works, only because he carried this truth within him, was himself this truth. He is *the* bearer of the Spirit of Truth for our time, of which Christ spoke in his farewell address in the Gospel of John, saying that this Spirit of Truth would come over humanity;[183] this actually came to pass on Whitsun morning.

This does not mean that Rudolf Steiner is the only bearer of the Spirit of Truth. It is particularly through him that we have knowledge of the other great initiates who were also bearers of this Spirit of Truth, which is the true spirit of Christ.[184] However, for our time of the consciousness soul and for the Michael-epoch in which we live, Rudolf Steiner is *the* bearer, *the* messenger of the Spirit of Truth.[185]

Looking further at Rudolf Steiner's life, we find an unbelievable, uninterrupted consistency with which he continually unfolded the anthroposophical impulse after the Christmas Conference. From where did he receive the sheer inexhaustible energy with which he worked? Already in the crisis-year 1923 he pointed in the course of the internal preparation for the Christmas Conference to the source from which this singular energy, which can overcome all, arises. It is of purely Michaelic nature. Rudolf Steiner formulated this in September 1923 in Vienna in a wonderful hymn for Michaelic faithfulness, for the loyalty which he himself showed especially after the Christmas Conference in absolute consistency and, as we will later see, maintained until the last breath of his life.

Already in May 1924 in Paris, Rudolf Steiner said in this regard that through the Christmas Conference a new alliance was forged with those spiritual powers—yes, with Michael himself and the hierarchical spirits serving him—which had led the Anthroposophical Movement in the spiritual world from the beginning.[186]

Then he reported in July 1924 in Arnhem about his own promise that he made to the spiritual world at the Christmas Conference, and added that this promise will be inviolably fulfilled.[187] Thus, Rudolf Steiner's life after the Christmas Conference until his crossing of the threshold on 30 March 1925, was nothing other than the pure expression of this steadfast loyalty regarding the promise that he made not to human beings, but to Michael himself.

Certainly Rudolf Steiner, like Benedictus in the Mystery Dramas, was one who on his pilgrim-path into the spiritual worlds had reached the stage at which he was permitted to serve spiritual beings with his counsel.[188] Of course he also did this previously, but through the Christmas Conference he now became to a still greater extent an advisor to Michael, the Time Spirit.[189]

Now, however, this hymn, which is likewise an expression of the pure Michael-power that radiated especially brightly through Rudolf Steiner during the last months of his earthly life, should be cited. It is a statement that brings to clarity what Rudolf Steiner actually exemplified—one might say both inherently, and also through his exceedingly spiritual activity following the Christmas Conference—in order to give us an example through which we may learn what it actually means to work out of the real Michael-force on the Earth: 'This ability to rise to the point at which thoughts about spirit can grip us as powerfully as can anything in the physical world, this is Michael power. It is confidence in the ideas of spirit—given the capacity for receiving them at all—leading to the conviction: I have received a spiritual impulse, I give myself up to it, I become the instrument for its execution. First failure—never mind! Second failure—never mind! A hundred failures are of no consequence, for no failure is ever a decisive factor in judging the truth of a spiritual impulse whose effect has been inwardly understood and grasped. We have full confidence in a spiritual impulse, grasped at a certain point of time, only when we can say to our self: My hundred failures can at most prove that the conditions for realizing the impulse are not given me in this incarnation; but that this impulse is right I can know from its own nature.' And now comes something entirely surprising: 'And if I must wait a hundred incarnations for the power to realize this impulse, nothing can convince me of the efficacy or impotence of any spiritual impulse but its own nature. If you will imagine this thought developed in the human soul [*Gemüt*] as a great confidence in spirit, if you will consider that a person can cling firm as a rock to something he has seen to be spiritually victorious, something he refuses to relinquish in spite of all outer opposition—then you will have a conception of what the Michael power, the Michael being, really demands of us; for only then will you comprehend the nature of the great confidence in the spirit. We may leave in abeyance some spiritual impulse or other, even for a whole incarnation; but once we have grasped it we must never waver in cherishing it within us, for only thus can we preserve it for subsequent incarnations. And when confidence in spirit will in this way have established a frame of mind to which this spiritual substance appears as real as the ground under our feet—the ground without which we could not stand—then we shall have in our soul [*Gemüt*] a feeling of what Michael really wants of us' (GA 223, 28 September 1923).[190]

In light of this statement, when we look back at the last months of Rudolf Steiner's life, we find how even on his sickbed he continued with everything that was still possible for him in exactly this unshakeable devotion. The chapters of his autobiography *The Course of My Life* continued to appear in the weekly newsletter; the *Leading Thoughts* and the accompanying articles that were given in order to hold the life of the Society together and give it a spiritual-Michaelic direction were written until the end, and published in the *Mitteilungsblatt*. Two of these articles even appeared after his death. Thus, they were like a greeting, like a last wave goodbye of the spiritual teacher from beyond the threshold, as though Rudolf Steiner were still here continuing on with his work.

The same faithfulness was carried forward by him with regard to the Anthroposophical Society and the School of Spiritual Science.[191] We know that in our circles, rumours are continually stirred up and untested statements brought into circulation about what Rudolf Steiner is reported to have said to the Stuttgart district attorney Bruno Krüger in relation to an alleged failure of the Christmas Conference and the Society. The exact circumstances of this real or alleged statement are, however, not known.[192] We also do not know what Rudolf Steiner really said to the eurythmist Ina Schuurman in passing, which she had understood as a statement about the failure of the Society and the Christmas Conference.

For it would have been very odd if Rudolf Steiner had imparted something so decisive to some people, who at that time played no particular role in the Anthroposophical Society, and at the same time withheld this crucial information from his closest colleagues and esoteric pupils Marie Steiner, Ita Wegman, Albert Steffen and others, so that they would continue to live in totally false conviction, as though everything would still proceed in the sense of the Christmas Conference (which then would no longer have been the case). One may not, in any case, impute such a thing to Rudolf Steiner.[193] In addition, the first mutual publication of the Executive Council, which was directed after Rudolf Steiner's death to all members of the Anthroposophical Society, testifies that they wanted to work together entirely in the sense of the esoteric impulse of the Christmas Conference.[194] That this intention could no longer be maintained due to inner conflicts with one another is a separate matter. However, the will to tread this spiritual path consistently was present in the Executive Council from the beginning.

This is not a matter of mere opinion opposed to opinion, or of one unsubstantiated narrative contrary to another; rather in this case we are dealing with irrefutable facts, available to us as unambiguous statements in documents written by Rudolf Steiner himself. Some of these are published at the end of a book that Peter Selg and I co-authored on the topic of the Christmas Conference.[195] Today one need only look into the archive of the Goetheanum to discover the way in which membership in the Society and the School of Spiritual Science was handled before Rudolf Steiner's death. For as long as he lived, Rudolf Steiner, as the first chairman of the Anthroposophical Society, personally admitted people, signing their pink cards with his own hand.[196] He didn't allow anyone else to do this for him. The same was true of membership in the School of Spiritual Science, in that Rudolf Steiner, as esoteric director, signed all blue cards with his own hand. Only by means of his signature—be it on the pink or the blue card— was the person in question from that moment on a member of the Anthroposophical Society or a member of the School of Spiritual Science.

If one follows further the date until which Rudolf Steiner accepted people into the School of Spiritual Science, and discovers that he conducted such admissions himself until *two days before his death*, then it becomes clear that the School was a full reality for him until the end. It follows that the Society also possessed this reality for him, because according to his own words the School is 'the soul of the Anthroposophical Society'.[197] Consequently, the Christmas Conference also retained complete reality for Rudolf Steiner. If he had considered it a failure, then the Society and School of Spiritual Science founded by him would naturally have become meaningless.[198]

If one reads, in the archives of the Goetheanum, the applications of people who at that time wanted to become members of the School, one will see that Rudolf Steiner read and evaluated all applications until the last days of his life, also after 8 February.[199] Thus he wrote—usually he did so with pencil—on one application: 'Must still wait'. This was a person from Norway, who had only been a member of the Society for one-and-a-half years. Rudolf Steiner had, however, clearly explained: A person must wait two years.[200] Further, on another long and somewhat confusing application was written: 'Must be researched in Stuttgart'. Rudolf Steiner wanted to have more information about this person in order to make his decision. And on a third application he wrote in large letters across the entire page: 'Yes!' with exclamation mark.[201]

If one considers still more precisely *up until when* Rudolf Steiner continued signing blue cards, then the reality of the situation becomes even more evident. In the register are the exact dates on which the persons in question were accepted into the School, and that means exactly when Rudolf Steiner, on his sickbed in the studio, personally signed the cards in question. Only after he signed was the new member entered into the register. In the Goetheanum Archive, one finds the list concerned. Here are a few excerpts from it:

14 March 1925—five people accepted into the School,
15 March 1925—three admissions . . .

Here one must visualize to himself the situation at that time very precisely. Rudolf Steiner hadn't been holding Class Lessons for a long time. Perhaps he already suspected in these last weeks what was coming, namely that he would soon have to leave the Earth. Nevertheless, he admits these people personally into the First Class, reads all applications himself, writes notes on them, signs the cards—and all of this precisely during the time when he can no longer raise himself out of bed due to his decreasing physical strength.

The School admissions, however, continue:

17 March 1925—two admissions
18 March 1925—one admission
25 March 1925—eight admissions
26 March 1925—one admission

And the last group of admissions comes only one-and-a-half days before he parted from the Earth. *Thirteen blue cards* were brought to him on this day: 28 March 1925—thirteen admissions due to the completed signature of Rudolf Steiner.

So one does not need to rely on rumours, because we are dealing with irrefutable facts, regardless of what some anthroposophists think about it today. It is decisively evident that the Christmas Conference, and the Society and School of Spiritual Science founded through it, were a full reality for Rudolf Steiner until the end—according to his promise, which remained inviolable, and on the basis of his alliance with the good forces of the spiritual world. There can also be no doubt that Rudolf Steiner, as the only justified director of the Michael School on the Earth, took this confidence, this unwavering loyalty with him into the spiritual world after his death. For everything he said he had also in fact lived, because in him truth and person flowed together into a unity. Therein lies the essential secret of his biography.

In conclusion, let us look once again at our present time and also at what Rudolf Steiner has left us as the central motif of the Christmas Conference. This motif is just as simple as it is difficult to accomplish. For one can only summarize the being of the Christmas Conference—in any case from a certain point of view—in one single appeal: 'More anthroposophy!'[202]

What lies before us in anthroposophy? This is something we must really call to mind. In anthroposophy we have the most modern endeavour that a person can possibly imagine in our time. To be sure, the most modern not in the sense of various fashion trends or styles, which are considered so today but in 20 or 50 years will be totally different; rather anthroposophy is actually—as Rudolf Steiner spoke of it in 1913 in London—'the gift of Michael'[203] to mankind, which means a gift of the Time Spirit. What can be more modern than the gift of the Time Spirit to his epoch—which will continue still for several hundred years and even beyond—than the path towards a conscious collaboration between human beings and the spiritual hierarchies? What could be more modern than that?

And how does it stand with respect to the present path to the etheric Christ? Rudolf Steiner said in this regard that anthroposophy is a new language which we must learn, no matter how difficult it is, in order to speak with the etheric Christ in the spiritual world.[204] Christ's etheric return will still last 3,000 years,[205] and after that will follow two higher manifestations of Christ, of which we have knowledge only from anthroposophy. Here we must seriously ask ourselves again: What could be more modern than the language—which, as with every foreign language, we must naturally make an effort to learn, whether or not one speaks German—through which we can then speak with the Being Who has given the Earth its highest meaning?[206] Here it is a matter of the meaning of the Earth and the entire evolution of humanity![207] What, then, is more modern? I cannot imagine anything more modern.

Then we must look at the founding of the Michael School. What can be more modern than the path through these 19 Class Lessons, which leads us to the innermost being of man. It is the path on which, for the first time in human history, the most deep-seated being of a person, the true human essence, is fathomed not only in an earthly way—as is discussed today in parliaments and lecture halls with regard to freedom and human rights—but cosmically; whereby it becomes evident that every person, no matter to which folk he belongs, has a cosmic significance. Here it is a matter of a very concrete path to the cosmic being of a person, to the true dimension of the human 'I', which becomes ever clearer on the path of the 19 Class Lessons.

One can also say: The secret of the human 'I' in its connection with the spiritual cosmos, the nine Hierarchies and the creative Logos itself is given to us in the course of the 19 Class Lessons, and therewith the intended purpose and goal of mankind on Earth, which consists in the full unfolding of the individual human 'I'.[208] What can be more future-oriented or modern than this? All of this is so modern, even more than modern, because it comes to us not from the past but from out of the future, giving us a firm inner foundation and orientation for the direction in which our present development must be guided.

Likewise, today anthroposophy gives the only relevant answer to the question of how the various miseries, difficulties and needs of our time can be overcome. This will, however, only be possible when we remain true and strive purposefully towards the true being of man, towards the meaning of the Earth and towards what gives us certainty and orientation in knowledge: that is, when we take responsibility for all of this just as unshakably and devotedly as Rudolf Steiner did himself, and certainly still does.

One can say much more about this. Unfortunately, the late hour of this evening does not allow it.

Thus, one must really come to recognize what spiritual treasures we actually hold in our hands with anthroposophy. If we do not see this, the fault lies not in anthroposophy, but only in ourselves. In order to bring this fully to consciousness, one need only look at Rudolf Steiner—at how all that he lived is exemplary for us, above all in the last months of his life before crossing the threshold.

Then Rudolf Steiner crossed over to the other side of the threshold, in the spiritual world. Now has the man arrived, who had lived consciously in the spiritual world for more than one-third of his life—now he has returned to his spiritual home. Because the true being of every person is of a spiritual nature,[209] Rudolf Steiner can be for all of us—if we truly want this—much closer to us than was possible during the time he dwelt on Earth, so long as we fulfil the conditions for this! Rudolf Steiner is always prepared to be there for us and to help us.[210]

This we know from the Mystery Dramas, where Benedictus reveals that he must accompany every one of his students who, consciously or unconsciously, received the light of higher knowledge from his spiritual research.[211] Precisely the same thing can be said of Rudolf Steiner. He is spiritually connected with every one of his students, provided that they want this. If we follow Rudolf Steiner in our will and deeds, then he continues to be connected with the Anthroposophical Society.[212]

Actually, there have always been enough members in this worldwide Society who, despite all of the conflicts and difficulties through which it has gone, have always done this. But it must become a reality above all here at the Goetheanum. For the Goetheanum is the place where this relation to Rudolf Steiner must be sought and maintained especially intensively, where this relation should live in an exemplary fashion, as well as become visible for others who come from far away. They too should be able to feel in this home, which Rudolf Steiner has given us, that his spirit is still present here.

Therefore in this place Rudolf Steiner must be defended earnestly and courageously against all slanderous and untruthful attacks, which were carried out in the world above all on the occasion of his 150th birthday. Where, if not here at the Goetheanum, must Rudolf Steiner be defended without compromise—for the sake of his dignity, for the sake of our dignity, dear friends!

In closing, let us look at this wonderful portrait of Rudolf Steiner.[213] A person can ask himself what reason anthroposophists would have for setting up a photograph of Rudolf Steiner or hanging one on the wall. Naturally there is here, as everywhere, much of a 'human, all-too-human' nature, sentimentality and so forth. However, one can find yet a deeper reason to do this. Many people have perhaps experienced for themselves upon seeing a picture of Rudolf Steiner for the first time, that they immediately felt: Such a face is not to be found anywhere else in the world. For the strength and purest spirituality that emanates from these unique facial features can never be forgotten! Through it shines not only the personal aspect of this man, who lived on the Earth from the 19th into the 20th century, but also something entirely objective, something much greater, something of the future, which can be of significance for every human being in the world.

What is concerned here is the real Michael-force, which, when strongly enough present in a person, is active from the spiritual through the soul, and into the physical body.[214] Through this the physical body is altered. The seal of the spirit is impressed upon such a person. And this comes to expression primarily in the person's face. This happens perhaps not in one incarnation, but after two, three, ten or 100 incarnations. Thereby, in the normal course of a human being's development the face becomes a mirror-image of the spirit, which however, in such an individual as Rudolf Steiner, occurred directly in this incarnation—as an example for us all.

Already in our time we begin to move towards the decisive separation of humanity, in which two groups will gradually arise: those who take up the spirit so that it transforms the physical body, and those who reject it. That is the single difference, and it will retain its validity throughout the entire future of human evolution. All other differences among people will be a thing of the past. In this sense Rudolf Steiner speaks of those people who already today begin to receive the spirit into themselves, as true 'Michaelites'.[215] He says further that in the future they will carry upon their physical body this seal of the Michael spirit, which will be revealed primarily in their countenance.[216]

Therefore, we are justified in being moved when we contemplate a photograph of Rudolf Steiner. For looking at us is a human being in whom truth has assumed concrete, visible form, and from which the earthly personality can no longer be separated—rather out of which shines towards us, through the characteristics of this face, the future of all mankind as the light of truth and spirit. This is then the true humanity, which will one day bear in their countenance the seal of the spirit, the seal of Michael-Christ. Rudolf Steiner bore it already in his incarnation in the 20th century. This seal of the spirit is what moves us so greatly when we look at his face.

Now for this photograph standing before us there is an unusual story. It was Fritz Hass from Munich who asked Rudolf Steiner in 1907 whether he might photograph him in a state of spiritual research. Surprisingly, Rudolf Steiner was in agreement with this. That is how this very special portrait of Rudolf Steiner came about.[217]

At this time, I would like to allow myself to comment how deeply it pains me that this special portrait had to be brought into this auditorium from out of the still-unfinished back staircase of the Goetheanum. It hung there for many months as an entirely lost exhibit, banished to this unworthy place, and surrounded by nothing but empty picture frames which were likewise suspended as museum-pieces. This portrait does not belong in a back staircase, but in this Great Hall [extensive applause]. And I very much hope that after this lecture it will not be banished again to this unfinished staircase, but rather worthily displayed in this House of Rudolf Steiner or returned to its owner in Holland, where it will surely be treated more worthily than has so far been the case here in the House of Rudolf Steiner.

I would like to close this lecture with two quite special verses. First, I will read a poem by Christian Morgenstern, which is dedicated to Rudolf Steiner; and at the end a meditation to the dead, during which I would like to ask you to stand. For the relation to the dead, and above all the relation to Rudolf Steiner, are among the most important tasks of our Society.[218] The period of the sixth cultural epoch—of which Rudolf Steiner once said that no decision, including those of a social-political nature should be made without first having agreement from the dead—no longer lies 'beyond the mountains'.[219] In this sense it belongs to the great task of our Society, and especially this building, to intensively cultivate the relationship to the dead.[220]

In order to round off this theme of Rudolf Steiner for the evening, there should be brought forward an example of a person who during Rudolf Steiner's lifetime had no primitive, naïve or childish devotion to him, but was one of his very few pupils who before coming to anthroposophy already enjoyed great recognition in the external world: Christian Morgenstern (1871 to 1914). As a mature person and well-known poet he brought to expression—already standing on the threshold of death—his great reverence for Rudolf Steiner in these wonderful lines, thus testifying that his encounter with Rudolf Steiner was the most important, the most precious event in his life,[221] the consequences of which would extend far beyond a single earthly life.

> Just as a person, on a cloudy day, forgets the sun—
> Which however shines and gleams endlessly—
> So may one forget yours on a gloomy day.
> Only again and ever again
> To find, shaken, even blinded
> How inexhaustibly on and on and on
> Your sun spirit
> Shines upon us dark wanderers.[222]

We end this evening with Rudolf Steiner's verse for the dead,[223] during which we stand:

> Spirits ever watchful, guardians of these souls,
> May your servants carry
> Our souls' petitioning love
> To the human beings entrusted to your care,
> That united with your power
> Our prayer may radiate with help
> To those souls, whom our love is seeking.

Afterword

> 'Why do you distance yourself
> so much from Rudolf Steiner?'
> *Ita Wegman*[224]

As conclusion to the content of my lecture, I still want to point out the special reason why I have closed the anniversary of Rudolf Steiner's death this year with the verse by Christian Morgenstern. In order to make this more understandable, I shall go into some detail about Christian Morgenstern's special individuality and poetic work.

He was not only one of the most outstanding anthroposophists and deepest esoteric pupils of Rudolf Steiner, but further, was one of the few anthroposophists who, before his acquaintance with Rudolf Steiner, held a firm place in the general world of culture, which paid him proper tribute. Thus, before he became an anthroposophist, Christian Morgenstern was already a well-known poet with a style and depth which in the German-speaking culture is comparable only with Rainer Maria Rilke, or in a Russian connection with Andrei Belyi (who to this day is characterized as a Russian James Joyce).

Perhaps just because he was completely independent and firmly anchored in the cultural world as person and artist, is it so significant that at the end of his life Christian Morgenstern brought to expression the deepest reverence for Rudolf Steiner, particularly in the book of poems *We Have Found a Path*. For it is indeed the case that the higher an individuality ascends in his inner development and thereby is stable in his own 'I', the more he possesses the capability to show an even higher person full recognition—which is free, open devotion, because it is well-founded in knowledge. Christian Morgenstern's respect towards his friend and teacher Rudolf Steiner was of just this kind: a reverence that bore within it absolute sovereignty and independence, which Christian Morgenstern undoubtedly possessed as person and famous German-speaking poet. Rudolf Steiner received and affirmed this public recognition from his pupil and friend Christian Morgenstern wholeheartedly, with great thankfulness and joy. One could say: It is hard to imagine something more beautiful and future-oriented than the spiritual friendship between Rudolf Steiner and Christian Morgenstern.

If one wanted to look for a parallel to this, it could perhaps only be found in the friendship between Goethe and Schiller,[225] which was like a new being coming to birth in the spiritual world. Rudolf Steiner reported about this: 'What we have in Goethe and Schiller is not only Goethe and Schiller, but we have a third thing: Goethe *plus* Schiller. Whoever follows the course of spiritual life sees in this *a being*, which could only come about when in selfless friendship, out of mutual respect, something unfolds that exists as a new being beyond the individual personality' (GA 51, 28 January 1905; italics Rudolf Steiner).

Already in our training book, *Knowledge of the Higher Worlds: How is it Achieved?*, Rudolf Steiner points out that the higher the pupil ascends on the spiritual path, the more conscious he becomes of the fact that there have been and will be individualities who are far more advanced than himself, because they preceded him on his spiritual path long ago.[226] If a person wants to enter into relationship with them (and this is indispensable for all further development), then this is only possible by generating a real reverence in the soul.

Here lies, however, an objective problem and a trial for every person striving for the spiritual: Only a mature and strongly grounded 'I' can in this sense express reverence to a still higher individuality without thereby losing himself.[227] If the 'I' is not strong enough, it cannot maintain itself. In order to avoid this problem, the weak 'I' defends itself in such a way that, where true respect would be appropriate, criticism is practised or antipathy (in extreme cases even hate) is developed. Therefore, in our time unbridled irreverence is brought to bear on what is worthy of veneration, not—as a superficial person may well imagine—through the strength and independence of one's own 'I', but precisely through one's weakness.

If the 'I' really is strongly filled with the spiritual force of anthroposophy, then there arises something like this wonderful friendship between Christian Morgenstern and Rudolf Steiner.

An even higher level, however, was attained by the deep reverence which Rudolf Steiner carried in his soul and cultivated for the other great teachers of humanity—some of whom, during his last incarnation on Earth, he had met in the physical body and others only in the spiritual world. Friedrich Rittelmeyer reports in this regard: 'I will never forget the look with which Rudolf said about one of these two spiritual individualities: "That was a very important personality!" His eyes followed after him for a long time. And in this gaze was the respect which one great knower pays to another.'[228]

Rudolf Steiner further reported that Christian Morgenstern had, as no other of his pupils, received the Christ impulse from anthroposophy into his soul. 'In that he [Christian Morgenstern] took up the anthroposophical teaching, in that he connected himself with this anthroposophical training to such an extent that it really became the spiritual life-blood of his heart and soul, he had also taken up this teaching in his soul in such a way that for him this anthroposophical teaching contained within it the substance of Christ. He had received it together with the Christ being. The Christ, as He lives in our movement, was transmitted to his soul at the same time.'[229] This penetration of the most internal being of his 'I' with the Christ-force had become so real and powerful in Christian Morgenstern at the time of his death that, according to Rudolf Steiner's spiritual research, through the posthumous path of his friend, Christian Morgenstern's entrance into the spiritual world was for it a great, even 'epochal', event. 'One can say, my dear friends, that the entrance into the spiritual world of the soul incorporated in Christian Morgenstern was such an event for these spiritual worlds that in a certain sense (if I may use a prosaic expression) it brought about an epoch in these spiritual worlds.'[230] Following this, Christian Morgenstern's greatness and significance could unfold so wonderfully after death that his soul became a teacher and leader in the spiritual world of such individualities as Fichte, Schelling and Hegel, who without his guiding help could have found no further path in their after-death existence.[231]

Thus, Christian Morgenstern was for Rudolf Steiner a shining example of what it really means to be a true representative of anthroposophy, which his friend brought to expression with his entire being not only on Earth, but also after his death for the dead and likewise for the higher Hierarchies.

When the pupil (in this case one of the most outstanding) reveals himself so powerfully in the spiritual world and can be active in it so extensively, what significance must we therefore connect with the moment when the great teacher himself, Rudolf Steiner, on 30 March 1925, around 10:00 in the morning, crossed the threshold to the spiritual world—where he was undoubtedly received, as one of the first, by Christian Morgenstern, who would have been witness to the sheer unimaginable significance which Rudolf Steiner's appearance had and still has in the spiritual world. If Rudolf Steiner was already so great in his earthly life—which we can gather from the entire nature of anthroposophy—how much greater and more significant was his individuality as, now no longer limited by the barriers of the physical body, it began to work in the spiritual world, surrounded by all of its deceased pupils who had already known his true greatness on Earth and therefore, out of their strong and independent 'I', harboured and cultivated the deepest reverence for their teacher.

For those anthroposophists, however, who still have inner problems with a free veneration, stemming from knowledge, for Rudolf Steiner as their spiritual teacher, I would like still, as a possibility, to display for them the best examples of this freely generated reverence, in pointing to a series of biographies that Peter Selg, along with numerous basic studies regarding Rudolf Steiner's work, has published in recent years. These biographies convey an insight into how Rudolf Steiner's most important pupils—every one of whom was a strong, 'I'-enhanced and above all independently creative personality, whose achievements in the service of anthroposophy we all remember still today—also cultivated in their souls the deepest respect for him, which was so pure and selfless that their sovereignty, freedom and exceptional self-consciousness was not thereby in the least impaired. From a far larger offering, I want to mention the following books by Peter Selg:

Christian Morgenstern, Sein Weg mit Rudolf Steiner [His Path with Rudolf Steiner], Stuttgart 2008.
Michael Bauer, Ein esoterischer Schüler Rudolf Steiners [An Esoteric Pupil of Rudolf Steiner], Dornach 2006.
Marie Steiner, Aufbau und Zukunft des Werkes von Rudolf Steiner [The Structure and Future of Rudolf Steiner's Works], Dornach 2006.
Ita Wegman, Erinnerung an Rudolf Steiner [Remembering Rudolf Steiner] (Ed. P. Selg), Arlesheim 2009.
Albert Steffen, Begegnung mit Rudolf Steiner [Meetings with Rudolf Steiner], Dornach 2009.
Elizabeth Vreede, 1879–1943, Arlesheim 2009.
Edith Maryon, Rudolf Steiner und die Dornacher Christus-Plastik [Rudolf Steiner and the Dornach Christ-Sculpture], Dornach 2006.
Willem Zeylmans van Emmichoven, Anthroposophie und Anthroposophische Gesellschaft im 20. Jahrhundert [Anthroposophy and the Anthroposophical Society in the 20th Century], Arlesheim 2009.
Karl Schuberts Beziehung zu Rudolf Steiner [Karl Schubert's Relationship to Rudolf Steiner], Arlesheim 2011.

Above all, however, his large, three-volume biography of Rudolf Steiner should be mentioned: *Rudolf Steiner, 1861–1925, Lebens- und Werk-*

geschichte [*A History of his Life and Work*]. With this great achievement, Peter Selg has salvaged the dignity of all anthroposophists on the occasion of the 150th anniversary of Rudolf Steiner's birth. For with this book not only are the most pretentious opponents of Rudolf Steiner and anthroposophy in the world today dealt with, but out of our own ranks a positive answer has been given—and in a form which demonstrates that one can indeed today achieve a mature relation towards Rudolf Steiner, as was the case for his above-mentioned pupils, and which will remain for all future times the only appropriate means of regard for this high Master. May this book by Peter Selg, which appeared via Verlag des Ita Wegman Institutes, become a proper training book, especially for younger anthroposophists, for how a person in our time can build a real relationship in his own soul to Rudolf Steiner as his personal spiritual teacher.

I would like to close this Afterword with two further verses by Christian Morgenstern, which point again to Rudolf Steiner's greatness as well as to the singularity of his work, which we as anthroposophists are called upon to care for, cultivate and stand up for on the Earth—especially here at the Goetheanum, in this House of Rudolf Steiner.

In the first verse, Christian Morgenstern—who, as one of the most important German-speaking poets of the 20th century, possessed a special sensitivity towards the being of the word, towards *how* a person speaks—has visualized for us his impressions of a lecture by Rudolf Steiner that he heard:

> He spoke. And as he spoke there appeared in him
> The Zodiac, Cherubim and Seraphim
> The sun star, the movement of the planets
> From place to place.
> All this sprang from his voice,
> Beheld like cosmic space with lightning speed,
> The whole heaven seemed to descend
> Through his word.[232]

This is the way in which Christian Morgenstern experienced Rudolf Steiner's speaking. And only through the force of his deep love and free, upright devotion, with which he approached Rudolf Steiner, was the being of the teacher—about whom he wrote in this verse—revealed to him. Before him stood a person who was completely connected with the power of the Word, the Logos, and spoke out of it.

With the same intensity, Christian Morgenstern experienced Rudolf Steiner's lectures captured stenographically. By reading the printed word he was able to develop the same relationship to Rudolf Steiner's spiritual being as was possible for him through the spoken word. What a legacy for us all, because today we are entirely dependent on the printed word!

> Your work leads to beauty;
> For beauty streams in
> Through all the revelations
> That it gives us.
> From human sufferings
> To ever higher harmonies
> You release a whirling sensation
> Until it joins
> With the harmony
> Of the inestimable proclaimer of GOD
> And HIS ungraspable radiance
> Resonates in loving light
> Of everlasting life . . .
> Coming from beauty,
> Your work
> Leads to beauty.[233]

Christian Morgenstern wrote this poem after the lecture of the Helsingfors cycle of 1912, *The Spiritual Beings in the Heavenly Bodies and in the Kingdoms of Nature* (GA 136), for which he could no longer be present due to his health condition. It is, therefore, precisely for this reason an especially valuable example of how even today—simply by reading Rudolf Steiner's lectures, if one only unfolds in his own soul the suitable attitude, as was the case with Christian Morgenstern—one can witness completely the singular beauty and true spiritual dimension of what has been expressed through this poem.

Due to his premature death, Christian Morgenstern was not able physically to take part in the Christmas Conference. All the more real and conscious, therefore, was his participation from the spiritual world. Along with Christian Rosenkreuz and his hosts,[234] he was also present supersensibly at that time in the *Schreinerei*.

And at the end of the Christmas Conference, when Louis Werbeck brought to expression his great thankfulness to Rudolf Steiner in the name of all participants, the words which he spoke in the culmination of his statement were formulated in quite the same sense as the last-cited poem by Christian Morgenstern—one could even say as though spoken by his soul:[235] 'Oh, my dear friends, we know the superhuman, the divine works through him!'

When one once becomes aware of the full esoteric dimension of the Christmas Conference,[236] then these words will be understood as no exaggeration, but as corresponding entirely to the truth.

Appendix: A Reflection on Peter Selg's Publication: *The Identity of the General Anthroposophical Society*[237]*

> 'The future rests upon the past.
> The past senses the future
> To give strength to the present ...'
> *Rudolf Steiner*[238]

Why do people study history? Why do they occupy themselves with their own biography, especially in later phases of life? Because from the history of humanity and by studying the biographies of great spirits, one can learn something that can prove to be of great help to one's own inner development.

Very often, however, one has the feeling that humanity can learn from its past failures only with great difficulty. But this should not really be the case within the Anthroposophical Society. For Rudolf Steiner has given us many spiritual keys with which to comprehend its nature and history, and which therefore place us in a position to accelerate its development.

For that reason, one can nearly suffer a shock when one reads the first of two lectures by Peter Selg, held in March of this year, in Basel and Dornach respectively. In it is contained a concise compilation of the problems of the Anthroposophical Society and of Rudolf Steiner's discussion of them during the crisis-year of 1923—or more precisely said, in the time between the burning of the first Goetheanum and the Christmas Conference.

Why is one so terrified of this straightforward confrontation with our own history? This is probably because, with regard to many of these problems, one must observe that they correspond precisely to the problems of our present time, some one hundred years later. From this, the question that appears in one's soul is: Are we, as yet, at all aware of our own history? Or to put it another way: Are we yet willing to study these issues so thoroughly, and internalize them so strongly, that we thereby become capable and ready to learn something from them? Or are we heading for a massive disaster, wherein we must repeat on a much larger

---

* Translated from the German by Thomas O'Keefe, with revisions by Simon Blaxland-de Lange.

scale the whole danger of which Rudolf Steiner warned us with such intensity and weighty words in 1923?

The real problem of this 'continual repetition of the same thing', however, lies still deeper: If our present situation in the Anthroposophical Society is so shamefully reminiscent of how it was in the year mentioned, how does it actually stand then with the Christmas Conference itself, through which was created the spiritual foundation for a solution with a spiritual dimension to all past and future problems of the Anthroposophical Society?

Is this central esoteric impulse of the Anthroposophical Movement better understood today than it was then? Or are we now swearing allegiance to this Christmas Conference almost automatically—as is common in a sect—without really understanding it? And is the necessary cognitive work not thereby replaced with a kind of creed?

Was the above-mentioned cognitive work in this most important area of anthroposophical esotericism really accomplished in the past years, for example, with any comparable diligence and scope of concern as was given to the widescale discussion on the question of the Constitution of the Anthroposophical Society at the turn of this century?[239]

Or has the necessary cognitive effort, which Rudolf Steiner probably also brought into connection with the fulfilment of the Michael Prophecy,[240] largely failed to come into being; and do we therefore find ourselves today once more in the situation of the year 1923, as if the Christmas Conference had never happened, or had in an esoteric sense become entirely repealed? Indeed, throughout his lifetime Rudolf Steiner had already spoken of the 'inner opposition' directed against himself, his task, and his intentions, from within the Anthroposophical Society.[241]

If one looks in this regard at the content of the second lecture by Peter Selg—held in the Great Hall of the Goetheanum during the General Meeting this year—one can form a picture from the facts cited there (which could be multiplied), that for the most part the Christmas Conference neither really lives within the Anthroposophical Society, nor actively radiates from the Goetheanum as its earthly centre.

Already in the year 1924, Rudolf Steiner said on two occasions that if the new esoteric impulse were not properly cared for by the Society in the following years, then the Being of the Christmas Conference could in the worst case even leave the Earth, because it would find no home within the people responsible for it.[242]

This would, however, under no circumstances mean that this unique deed of Rudolf Steiner's has been a failure or could not be carried in faithfulness within the souls of individual anthroposophists, so as to live and work further on Earth. Instead, the question that stands here is: *Can the esoteric impulse of the Christmas Conference, now and in the future, continue to be effective in the Anthroposophical Society, and above all in the Goetheanum?* And is the requisite understanding of this spiritual deed really at hand? When we raise these questions, we immediately stand in the midst of an intensive battlefield.

In his lecture, Peter Selg—alongside a fundamental, cognitively based discussion of the spiritual content of the Christmas Conference—indicated two essential conditions which alone make it possible to salvage the task mentioned. These are: the members' strengthened occupation with anthroposophy, and an intensive search for a spiritual relation to Rudolf Steiner in order to be able to continue his impulse.[243]

One can realize how pertinent these conditions are to the related problems of our time when one becomes aware of how anthroposophy, and above all anthroposophical Christology, has faded away from many institutions that were originally founded upon the anthroposophical impulse, and also from the Goetheanum itself, where in recent years this disappearance has been accompanied by an increasing disregard for Rudolf Steiner, as is described by Peter Selg in his publication. On the other hand, what is of crucial importance today is that, in the words of Peter Selg: 'The Goetheanum cannot be maintained in its present form, and an entirely different decisiveness for anthroposophy is needed at this place.'[244]

For it was intended by Rudolf Steiner from the very beginning that especially at the Goetheanum, as nowhere else in the world, human beings would be able to encounter anthroposophy in a pure and unadulterated way, and also to find its Christological core there. And after Rudolf Steiner's death, there should radiate with strength from this central place of his earthly work a true and unadulterated picture of the spiritual teacher himself, who in the first quarter of the 20th century founded anthroposophy upon the Earth as a modern science of the spirit. Further, only on the path of a freely won esoteric relation to Rudolf Steiner, as he works further in the spiritual world as a spiritual representative of humanity,[245] can the representation and carrying-into-the-world of anthroposophy be true and fruitful today.

'How do we stand *before* Rudolf Steiner today?'—This question, with which Peter Selg began his lecture in the Great Hall, is in our present time actually relevant and important as never before. This requires, however, that there would go forth from the Goetheanum an uncompromising and courageous representation of anthroposophy; and also that its creator would in all cases be openly defended when he, as in certain publications appearing in the world in the past year (and these were also mentioned by Peter Selg), is slandered and his image distorted and tarnished with lies.

Regarding this, one can find clear guidelines given by Rudolf Steiner himself in the year 1923: 'And for as long as we do not have the courage really [...] to look the *untruthfulness* in the eye, we will achieve nothing. And for this, I would like to say, courage is frequently lacking. One recoils—when one or another person in a certain position is indeed actually not permitted to lie, but lies nonetheless—at the thought of saying: "You have lied, it is not true; you simply lie, you do not speak the truth." So long as one does not look this in the eye, nothing will be achieved with regard to all the questions raised by our opponents.'[246] For 'the one thing that harms it [anthroposophy], is the lies of the opponents; not the refutations, but the lies of the opponents'. But it follows from this that when anthroposophists encounter these lies—many of which, regarding anthroposophy and above all its founder, have become common worldwide—and do not stand up against them with courage and decisiveness, then, whether they wish to or not, these anthroposophists work together with the opponents towards the destruction of anthroposophy.

Furthermore, as an anthroposophist, one must make oneself entirely clear about this: that in addition to the Michael School in the supersensible world, there worked at the same time and directly under the Earth's surface, a powerful anti-Michaelic School of Ahriman,[247] wherein human souls were being prepared to work in our time as merciless opponents of anthroposophy and Rudolf Steiner. And if as an anthroposophist one has up until now still not understood that it is above all in such cases, where anthroposophy has been distorted and Rudolf Steiner slandered, that Ahriman works as an author—then one has neither understood nor taken earnestly the relevant warnings of the spiritual teacher.[248] 'If [...] in response to the opposition nothing is done, then the mission of anthroposophy will fail', said Rudolf Steiner in this regard.[249] And if in the Anthroposophical Society—and above all at the Goetheanum—nothing or not enough is done in this direction, then this process of annihilation and disintegration will be yet further accelerated.

Both of these above-named conditions are inseparably bound together with the Being of the Christmas Conference. For they should on the one hand bring 'more anthroposophy' into the Anthroposophical Society;[250] and on the other hand, through this, bring about an entirely new relation between the pupils and their spiritual teacher, who has taken upon himself the karma of the Society.[251]

Only when these two conditions are cultivated and supported by the members—and especially at the Goetheanum—with all the strength at our disposal, can the Anthroposophical Society remain connected to the esoteric impulse of the Christmas Conference as its aim and future-oriented task.

In this sense, these lectures by Peter Selg are a strong and courageous call to the members of the Anthroposophical Society and to its leadership to come to recognize the tragedy of our present situation, and in these last moments to take hold of the necessary means for recovery. Then, through our renewed and conscious devotion towards anthroposophy and Rudolf Steiner in unbreakable loyalty and awareness, the danger that confronts the Anthroposophical Society today throughout the world may, with the spiritual help of its founder and out of the true and living impulse of the Christmas Conference, still be averted.

May this call for wakefulness from Peter Selg not fade away in vain among anthroposophists as 'a voice in the wilderness'.

Notes

GA = *Gesamtausgabe* or Collected Works of Rudolf Steiner. All GA page numbers refer to the German editions unless otherwise noted. A list of GA numbers and their English translations can be found on p. 127.

1. GA 286, p. 62.
2. GA 330, p. 54.
3. Quoted from Christoph Lindenberg, *Rudolf Steiner. Eine Chronik*. Stuttgart 1988, p. 330.
4. Ibid.
5. GA 28, p. 413.
6. GA 257, p. 60.
7. Ibid.
8. See in this regard especially the extensive study by Ekkehard Meffert, *Mathilde Scholl und die Geburt der Anthroposophischen Gesellschaft 1912/13* [Mathilde Scholl and the Birth of the Anthroposophical Society in 1912/13]. Dornach 1991, p. 219ff. and p. 448ff.
9. Michael Bauer, *Gesammelte Werke* [Collected Work]. 5 Vol., Ed. Christoph Rau, Stuttgart 1985–1997. Vol. 4, p. 82.
10. Quoted from J. E. Zeylmans van Emmichoven, *Willem Zeylmans van Emmichoven. An Inspiration for Anthroposophy*. Temple Lodge 2002, p. 80.
11. GA 257, p. 27.
12. GA 259, p. 77.
13. Ibid., p. 79.
14. Ibid., p. 80.
15. Ibid., p. 211.
16. GA 303, p. 326.
17. GA 259, p. 69.
18. GA 34, p. 196.
19. GA 96, p. 325.
20. GA 193, p. 158.
21. Ibid., p. 121.
22. GA 34, p. 344.
23. GA 263a [Correspondence between Rudolf Steiner and Edith Maryon], p. 102.
24. GA 257, p. 58.
25. GA 259, p. 69.
26. GA 231, p. 153.
27. GA 258, p. 144.

28. GA 257, p. 180.
29. GA 217, p. 62.
30. GA 257, p. 154.
31. GA 197, p. 85, italics added.
32. Ibid., p. 91.
33. GA 259, p. 381.
34. Ibid., p. 484.
35. GA 260a, p. 116.
36. Quoted from J. E. Zeylmans van Emmichoven, *Willem Zeylmans van Emmichoven. An Inspiration for Anthroposophy*. Temple Lodge 2002, p. 80.
37. GA 217a, p. 98.
38. GA 255b, p. 561.
39. GA 257, p. 68.
40. Ibid., p. 84.
41. GA 259, p. 301.
42. Ibid., p. 342.
43. Cf. Peter Selg, *The Path of the Soul after Death. The Community of the Living and the Dead as Witnessed by Rudolf Steiner in his Eulogies and Funeral Addresses*. SteinerBooks 2011.
44. GA 258, p. 141, lecture of 16 June 1923.
45. Ibid.
46. GA 259, p. 604.
47. Ibid., p. 254.
48. Cf. GA 258.
49. GA 257, p. 116.
50. Ibid., p. 120.
51. Cf. GA 258, p. 138; lecture of 16 June 1923.
52. Ibid.
53. GA 307, p. 253.
54. GA 259, p. 607.
55. Ibid.
56. Ibid., p. 670.
57. Ibid., p. 668.
58. Ibid., p. 473.
59. Ibid., p. 176.
60. GA 257, p. 137.
61. Quoted from Joachim C. Fest: *Hitler. Eine Biographie*. Frankfurt am Main, Berlin und Wien 1973, p. 208.
62. Rainer Maria Rilke, Letter to Lisa Heise, 2 February 1923. In: Rainer Maria Rilke, *Briefe zur Politik*. Ed. Joachim W. Storck. Frankfurt am Main und Leipzig 1992, p. 415.
63. Ita Wegman Archive.

64. With regard to the Mystery-background of Rudolf Steiner's decision, cf. especially the definitive study by J. Emanuel Zeylmans van Emmichoven: *Who Was Ita Wegman? A Documentation. Vol. 2—1925 until 1943*. Mercury Press 2005.
65. Ita Wegman Archive.
66. GA 259, p. 735.
67. GA 232, p. 224.
68. Cf. especially the comprehensive study by Sergei O. Prokofieff: *May Human Beings Hear It! The Mystery of the Christmas Conference*. Temple Lodge 2004 (as well as the secondary literature mentioned there).
69. GA 260, p. 64.
70. Ibid., p. 140.
71. Ibid., p. 53.
72. Ibid., p. 55.
73. Ibid., p. 142.
74. Ibid., p. 36.
75. GA 270a, p. 172.
76. GA 260, p. 92.
77. GA 260a., p. 115.
78. Ibid., p. 170.
79. Ibid., p. 207.
80. Ibid., p. 74f.
81. Ibid., p. 271.
82. GA 260, p. 37.
83. Ibid., p. 46; lecture of 24 December 1923, 11.15 am.
84. Ibid., p. 93f.; lecture of 26 December 1923, 10 am.
85. 22 November 1923. Quoted from *Rudolf Steiner und die Gründung der Weleda*. Ed. Alexander Lüscher. Contributions to the Rudolf Steiner's Collected Works No. 118/119. Dornach 1997, p. 182.
86. GA 260, p. 48; lecture of 24 December 1923, 11.15 am.
87. Ibid., p. 252.
88. Cf. the Appendix to Part I of this book.
89. GA 260a, p. 60.
90. Ibid., p. 30.
91. Ibid., p. 84.
92. Ibid., p. 68.
93. Ibid., p. 39.
94. Ibid., p. 86.
95. Ibid., p. 61.
96. Ibid., p. 63; 23 March 1924. [In English: *The Life, Nature and Cultivation of Anthroposophy*, p. 38.]
97. GA 259, p. 683.

98. GA 257, p. 194.
99. GA 26, p. 114ff.
100. GA 257, p. 194.
101. GA 259, p. 75.
102. Friedrich Hölderlin, 'Patmos'. In: *Sämtliche Werke* [Complete Works]. Vol. 2. Ed. Friedrich Beissner. Stuttgart 1951, p. 173.
103. Quoted from Walter Kugler, *Rudolf Steiner. Wie manche ihn sehen und andere wahrnehmen*. Stuttgart 2008, p. 111.
104. Notebook No. 74, 30 March 1941. Ita Wegman Archive.
105. Cf. Peter Selg, *Michael Bauer. Ein esoterischer Schüler Rudolf Steiners*. Dornach 2006, p. 117ff.
106. Michael Bauer, *Gesammelte Werke* [Collected Work]. Op. cit., Vol. 4, p. 180.
107. 'A person who has gained a real relationship to Steiner's mission cannot be crazy. For [Rudolf Steiner's] ideas are so outstanding in every regard compared with what is normally offered, that one can only admire and appreciate them when one truly understands. Still none of us can really grasp sufficiently the greatness and importance of his work; we are standing too close to it.' Michael Bauer: Letter to Ludwig Sauter, July 1913. In: Michael Bauer, *Gesammelte Werke* [Collected Work]. Op. cit., Vol. 5, p. 36.
108. Assya Turgenieff, *Was wird mit dem Goetheanumbau geschehen?* Basel 1956, p. 13.
109. Ibid., p. 31.
110. Michael Bauer, *Gesammelte Werke* [Collected Work]. Op. cit., Vol. 4, p. 179.
111. Miriam Gebhardt, *Rudolf Steiner. Ein moderner Prophet*. [Rudolf Steiner. A Modern Prophet.] Munich 2011, p. 9.
112. Ibid., p. 10.
113. Ibid., p. 116.
114. Ibid., p. 11.
115. Ibid., p. 343.
116. Ibid., p. 13.
117. Ibid., p. 14.
118. Ibid., p. 169.
119. Ibid., p. 129.
120. GA 259, p. 597.
121. GA 270a, p. 151.
122. GA 221, p. 139, lecture of 18 February 1923.
123. GA 170, p. 110.
124. Christian Morgenstern, 'Verantwortung' [Responsibility]. In: *Werke und Briefe* [Work and Letters]. Stuttgart Edition. Ed. Reinhardt Habel. Vol. II: Lyrik 1906–1916. Stuttgart 1992, p. 251.
125. Fritz Götte, 'In memoriam Frederik Willem Zeylmans van Emmichoven'.

In: *Mitteilungen aus der anthroposophischen Arbeit in Deutschland.* Weihnachten 1964, p. 266. Cf. also Peter Selg, *Willem Zeylmans van Emmichoven. Anthroposophie und Anthroposophische Gesellschaft im 20. Jahrhundert.* Arlesheim 2009, p. 149ff.
126. GA 217a, p. 99.
127. First published in: *Das Goetheanum. Wochenschrift für Anthroposophie* [Weekly Newsletter for Anthroposophy]. 2010; Issue 50: 1–4.
128. Peter Selg, *Rudolf Steiner und die Freie Hochschule für Geisteswissenschaft. Die Begründung der Ersten Klasse.* Arlesheim 2008, p. 35f. [In English: Peter Selg, *Rudolf Steiner and the School for Spiritual Science. The Foundation of the 'First Class'.* SteinerBooks 2012.]
129. GA 300c, p. 114.
130. Ibid., p. 115.
131. Ibid., p. 115f.
132. Ibid., p. 119.
133. Lilly Kolisko, *Eugen Kolisko. Ein Lebensbild.* Gerabronn–Crailsheim 1961, p. 90.
134. Rudolf Steiner to Lilly Kolisko. In: Lilly Kolisko, *Brief an Ita Wegman, 2 November 1924* [Letter to Ita Wegman]. Ita Wegman Archive.
135. On the significance of the Class Lessons for the Collegium of teachers, cf. Lilly Kolisko, *Brief an Ita Wegman, 2 November 1924.* Ibid. Likewise published in Johannes Kiersch, *A History of the School of Spiritual Science. The First Class.* Temple Lodge 2006, p. 71ff. and Peter Selg, *Rudolf Steiner and the School for Spiritual Science. The Foundation of the 'First Class'.* SteinerBooks 2012, p. 115.
136. Cf. GA 308, p. 93.
137. Rudolf Steiner Archive.
138. Cf. Peter Selg, *Helene von Grunelius und Rudolf Steiners Kurse für die jungen Mediziner. Eine biographische Studie.* Dornach 2003.
139. Regarding this topic, cf. Peter Selg, *'Die Medizin muss Ernst machen mit dem geistigen Leben'. Rudolf Steiners Hochschulkurse für die 'jungen Mediziner',* Dornach 2006.
140. Madeleine P. van Deventer, *Die anthroposophisch-medizinische Bewegung in den verschiedenen Etappen ihrer Entwicklung.* Arlesheim 1982, p. 28.
141. GA 270a, p. 149.
142. GA 270c, p. 162.
143. GA 316, p. 223.
144. Ibid., p. 73f.
145. Peter Selg, *Rudolf Steiner und die Freie Hochschule für Geisteswissenschaft. Die Begründung der Ersten Klasse.* Op. cit., p. 35f. [In English: Peter Selg, *Rudolf Steiner and the School for Spiritual Science. The Foundation of the 'First Class'.* SteinerBooks 2012.]

146. Regarding the 'Esoteric core of the Medical Section', its structure and tasks, Cf. GA 318, p. 165f and Peter Selg, *Die Briefkorrespondenz der 'jungen Mediziner'. Eine dokumentarische Studie zur Rezeption von Rudolf Steiners 'Jungmediziner'-Kursen.* Dornach 2005, p. 145ff.
147. Gottfried Husemann, 'Die Begründung der Christengemeinschaft'. In: *Erinnerungen an Rudolf Steiner.* Ed. Erika Beltle and Kurt Vierl. Stuttgart 1979, p. 311.
148. For a conception of the '*newly* founded' School of Spiritual Science based upon the Christmas Conference of 1923/24, Cf. Peter Selg, *Rudolf Steiner und die Freie Hochschule für Geisteswissenschaft. Die Begründung der Ersten Klasse.* Op. cit., p. 19ff. [In English: Peter Selg, *Rudolf Steiner and the School for Spiritual Science. The Foundation of the 'First Class'.* SteinerBooks 2012.]
149. GA 300c, p. 177.
150. GA 346, p. 44.
151. GA 233a, p. 134f.—Cf. in this regard the comprehensive study by Sergei O. Prokofieff: *The First Class of the Michael School and its Christological Foundations.* Dornach 2012.
152. GA 316, p. 220.
153. GA 270c, p. 151.
154. GA 260a, p. 77f.
155. Quoted from Peter Selg, 'The Identity of the General Anthroposophical Society'. In: Part I of this book, lecture of 30 March 2012, 'The Challenges of the Present and Future'.
156. The added remarks should indicate the background out of which my lecture was held, and how it is rooted in Rudolf Steiner's work and in connection with his pupils.
157. The photograph can be found on page 68 of this book. About the special history of its origin, please see further in this lecture.
158. This refers to the north staircase behind the stage, where the rough cement walls, steel reinforcements, and unfinished portions of the architecture (stairs, stair landings, etc.) remain. When today a person sets out to collect money for repairs that have become necessary for the Goetheanum building, he should also ask himself whether this building of great, world-architectural mastery shouldn't first of all be completed [before being repaired].
159. 'That which relates to me is considered within fairly wide circles of the Anthroposophical Society as a negligible quantity' (GA 259, 22 July 1923).
160. 'My dear friends, I have often said—though it perhaps appears to you unjustified—that there exists inner opposition within the Anthroposophical Society against what I often have to represent from out of the heart of anthroposophy' (GA 259, 17 June 1923). Regarding Rudolf Steiner's illness in his final two years of life, Ita Wegman wrote in her

notebook: 'A lack of understanding hinders. Illness likewise through incomprehension, through opposition' (quoted from Ita Wegman, ed. P. Selg, *Erinnerung an Rudolf Steiner*. Verlag des Ita Wegman Instituts, Arlesheim 2009, p. 42).

161. When now, after my lecture, a photograph of Rudolf Steiner is displayed at the Goetheanum in an entirely inappropriate room—where tickets used to be sold, and where today internet connections have been installed for visitors—and in which the most important thing that Rudolf Steiner accomplished in his life, namely *founding anthroposophy as spiritual science*, is not mentioned in the accompanying caption, then this is in no way relevant to the concerns raised in my lecture.

162. Peter Selg, 'The Identity of the General Anthroposophical Society', Preface. See Part I of this book.

163. Quoted from Marie Steiner, *Briefe und Dokumente vornehmlich aus ihrem letzten Lebensjahr*. Dornach 1981.

164. Quoted from J.E. Zeylmans van Emmichoven, *Who Was Ita Wegman? A Documentation. Vol. I—1876 until 1925*. Mercury Press 1995. Chapter: 'The Last Period with Rudolf Steiner'.

165. 'But we must for once begin with the real esotericism, now that we have more than two decades of preparatory work behind us [1902 to 1923]. Thus, the Christmas Conference could take place in Dornach, whereby the esoteric entered into the Society' (GA 240, 16 April 1924).—See also GA 240, 9 April 1924 and S.O. Prokofieff, *Die Esoterik der Anthroposophischen Gesellschaft*. Dornach 2012. ['The Esotericism of the Anthroposophical Society'—English translation forthcoming.]

166. See GA 260, 31 December 1923.

167. 'The Masters are not a protective wall against evil, rather they are leaders in the absorption of evil. We should not weed out evil, but take hold of it and use it in the sphere of good' (GA 264, p. 188).

168. 'This painful suffering, however, gave birth to this spirit which was poured out onto the disciples at Whitsun. Out of this pain was born the all-embracing cosmic love' (GA 148, 3 October 1913). On Whitsun morning the disciples knew 'that Jesus died on the cross and that this death was really a birth, the birth of that Spirit Who as all-embracing love had poured Himself into the souls of the disciples gathered at Whitsun' (GA 148, 2 October 1913).

169. GA 260a, 6 February 1914.

170. 'What was more or less previously an earthly affair [the Goetheanum]—was prepared, founded as earthly affair—this has been carried by the flames out into the world's expanses.' Thereafter, 'the matter of the Goetheanum is one of the vast ether, in which lives the spirit-filled wisdom of the world. It has been carried out, and we may permeate our-

selves with the Goetheanum-impulses as they come back to us from the cosmos' (GA 233a, 22 April 1924).
171. GA 260, p. 287.
172. In this regard see GA 202, 25 December 1910 and GA 233a, 12 January 1924.
173. See GA 131, 7 October 1911.
174. The first Class Lesson took place on 15 February 1924.
175. See GA 260, 15 December 1923.
176. In this regard, see more detail in S.O. Prokofieff, *The Foundation Stone Meditation. A Key to the New Christian Mysteries*. Temple Lodge 2006. Chapter 6: 'The Union of the Rosicrucian and Michael Streams in the Foundation Stone Meditation'.—In the lecture of 13 January 1924, Rudolf Steiner describes—what he said surely also has biographical implications—that a person brings to Michael today the results of his deeds, which are then evaluated as to whether they correspond to the 'world guidance of the cosmos' or not. If the former is the case, then Michael receives these deeds of the person into the spiritual world where they become cosmic deeds, i.e., as part of the Foundation Stone of the future cosmos. 'Thus, Michael carries that which is human earthly deed into the cosmos, so that it becomes cosmic deed' (GA 233a).
177. This refers to the cycle of ten lectures that I held in 2011 in the Goetheanum, on the occasion of Rudolf Steiner's 150th birthday.
178. Rudolf Steiner speaks about the experience of the higher 'I' through the spiritual meeting with the true Masters in GA 93, 18 October 1905.—In this regard see also S.O. Prokofieff, *Relating to Rudolf Steiner, and the Mystery of the Laying of the Foundation Stone*. Temple Lodge 2008. Chapter 4: 'A Path to Rudolf Steiner'.
179. 'There are children who look up with reverent awe to certain venerated persons. Their reverence for these people forbids them, even in the depths of their hearts, to admit any thought of criticism or opposition. Such children grow up into young men and women who feel happy when they are able to look up to anything that fills them with veneration. Many occult pupils come from the ranks of such children' (GA 10, Chapter: 'How is Knowledge of the Higher Worlds Achieved?' Section 1: *Conditions*).
180. Perhaps he would even have entered into the circle of His closest disciples, in place of Judas Iscariot.
181. Rudolf Steiner often spoke to Marie Steiner about the necessity of taking care that his work—especially after his death—be not separated from his name. She remembered it as follows: 'He spoke to me about the time when he would no longer be there, and when I would have to take responsibility for his work, also to ensure that his work for humanity would remain connected with his name. For few people would remain loyal to him; and

there was the danger that if his work were torn away from his name, it would become alienated from his original intentions. Then opposing powers would be able to seize the forces contained in it and make use of them for their own purposes' (Marie Steiner, 'Welches sind die Aufgaben des Nachlassvereins?', quoted from *Briefe und Dokumente vornehmlich aus ihrem letzten Lebensjahr*. Dornach 1981). He also spoke with Ita Wegman about this, which she recorded in the following statement: 'I only have to leave the physical plane, and if then the opposing powers would succeed in separating the content of anthroposophy from me, in the sense that the teachings are spread widely among the masses without knowledge of me, so that it becomes superficial—then would come to pass what the ahrimanic powers intend and strive for' (From the [*Das Goetheanum*] *Nachrichtenblatt*, 28 June 1925).

182. In the context of this description, one must also call to mind the fact that Rudolf Steiner characterized *devotion* as that force which primarily leads to the inner training and proper development of the consciousness soul. ('Thus, devotion will become the teacher of the consciousness soul.') This soul-quality consists of an intensified working of 'love and humility' in the human soul (GA 59, 28 October 1909). The full significance of devotion and reverence can be gathered from the fact that humanity has for several centuries been living in the epoch of consciousness-soul development (the fifth post-Atlantean cultural epoch). From this it is also understandable why Rudolf Steiner dedicated a full five-and-a-half pages to describing the development of this capacity in his book *Knowledge of the Higher Worlds: How is it Achieved?* (see GA 10).

183. 'And I will pray the Father, and He will give you another Comforter, the giver of spirit-courage, who will be with you for this whole earthly aeon, the Spirit of Truth. Not all people can receive Him. They do not see Him and do not recognize Him. But you know Him, for He guides you as a higher being above you, and He will enter your innermost heart' (John 14:16–17, J. Madsen Tr.).

184. In this sense, Rudolf Steiner speaks about Mani, the founder of Manichaeism: 'Mani, however, described himself as the "Paraclete", as the Holy Spirit promised by Christ to humanity. Now this should be interpreted to mean that he characterized himself as *one* incarnation of the Holy Spirit; he did not mean to say that he was the sole expression of the Holy Spirit' (GA 93, 11 November 1904; italics Rudolf Steiner). Here, by incarnation is to be understood a complete penetration of the high initiate with the Holy Spirit, Who then appeared in earthly manifestation through this person. This stage corresponds in Eastern mysticism to that of a Bodhisattva. Rudolf Steiner says in this regard: 'In the tradition of Near-East language, with regard to such a being as an incorporated Bodhisattva on Earth, one

would have said: He is "filled with the Holy Spirit"' (GA 114, 20 September 1909). Among those having achieved this high level of development, Rudolf Steiner named such individuals as Skythianos, Zarathustra (Master Jesus) and Christian Rosenkreuz. (See GA 113, 31 August 1909.)—Upon what path such a connection with the Holy Spirit is possible becomes evident from the description in *Theosophy* with regard to how a person today becomes a 'bearer of the Spirit Self' (called Manas in the East). 'The consciousness soul *lives in connection* with the truth that exists in oneself independently of any antipathy and sympathy. The Spirit Self bears within itself *the same* truth, but taken up into and enclosed by the "I"; individualized by it, and absorbed into the independent being of the person. It is through the eternal truth becoming thus individualized and bound up into one being with the "I" that the "I" itself attains to the eternal' (GA 9, Chapter I, Section 4: 'Body, Soul and Spirit'; italics Rudolf Steiner). Rudolf Steiner himself took precisely this path. This means that for him 'the eternal truth' was 'bound up *into one being* with his "I"'. About the connection between the Spirit Self and the Holy Spirit, Rudolf Steiner says in an early lecture: 'The Holy Spirit is called Spirit Self in my book *Theosophy*' (GA 96, 27 April 1907); and that means that the Spirit Self has a special relationship to the Holy Spirit. When the Spirit Self is really developed in a person—as was the case in the highest degree with Rudolf Steiner (however, only in the framework of how such development can occur already on Earth, for its full unfolding will only be possible on Jupiter)—then the Spirit Self in this person will become a faculty by means of which the Holy Spirit can be present in him, out of which the person is then able to work and his 'I' enabled to participate in the eternal. 'And when the "I" has already worked to some extent on the astral body, then something of Manas, something of the Holy Spirit is also present in the person. This Manas works in the person *through the outpouring of the Holy Spirit*' (ibid.) Rudolf Steiner was and is such a bearer of Manas (of the Spirit Self) 'through the outpouring of the Holy Spirit' for our time of the consciousness soul.

185. In this connection, the following remembrances of Countess Johanna von Keyserlingk from the time with Rudolf Steiner in Dresden in September 1919 are of significance: 'From these Dresden days the following has remained significant in my memory: As one can imagine, we were often occupied with the question: "Who is this mysterious Rudolf Steiner?" Because Mrs von Moltke now knew that I have clairvoyance, and Rudolf Steiner also communicated this to Marie Steiner and Miss Waller, she could not help considering my opinion about it. I said to her: "Rudolf Steiner's external figure seems to me like a sheath behind which a gleaming gold spirit-form emerges." Then I said: "He bears the force which Christ

promised He would send as the 'Comforter', who leads us in complete truth." Mrs von Moltke didn't reject these thoughts, but replied that she couldn't accept them; because Rudolf Steiner firmly refuses attributing "divinity" to his person by his pupils, he would definitely oppose them. So I asked her to somehow pose this question to Rudolf Steiner. She went to him and raised the question. I waited for her in the hotel and saw how she sank into the chair and said: "Yes, he confirmed what you said"' (Ed. A. Keyserlingk, *The Birth of a New Agriculture: Koberwitz 1924*. Temple Lodge 2000. Chapter: 'Encounters 1919 to 1921').

186. In Paris Rudolf Steiner literally said: 'But out of this we can hope that the forces of the alliance that we were allowed to make through the Christmas Conference with the good *spiritual powers* will be able in the future to defeat all of those opposing forces in the spiritual regions, which make use of human beings on Earth in order to achieve their impact—to drive all of these opposing forces from the field' (GA 260a, 23 May 1924).—That here and in other places throughout his lectures and writings after the Christmas Conference, the good 'spiritual powers' indicate above all Michael himself and the hierarchical spirits serving him, follows from another statement by Rudolf Steiner: 'Viewed from a supersensible perspective, the matter appears as follows: The *spiritual powers* that one can characterize with the name Michael, hold sway over ideas in the spiritual cosmos' (GA 26, article: 'The Condition of the Human Soul Before the Dawn of the Michael Age').

187. Rudolf Steiner said in Arnheim: 'There is in a certain sense also a promise to the spiritual world. This promise will be fulfilled in an inviolable manner' (GA 240, 18 July 1924).

188. In the first Mystery Drama, *The Portal of Initiation* (GA 14), Benedictus says:
    When on the soul's pilgrim path
    I had achieved this stage
    That gave me the honour
    To serve with my advice in the spiritual spheres.
    (Act 3)

189. Moreover, because the Christmas Conference was carried out entirely in the sense of the New Mysteries out of the spirit of Christ, Michael himself was from then on the 'Server of His Spirit'. Ita Wegman remembered this from a conversation with Rudolf Steiner while he was in his sick bed: 'And so the Mystery came about that extended further over Rudolf Steiner's life and activity until the time of his illness. Not only Michael expressed himself through him, but still far higher powers brought themselves to expression; Michael became the server of his spirit' (*An die Freunde*, article dated 20 September 1925, Arlesheim 1960). At this same time (autumn 1925) Ita Wegman noted for herself what that meant: 'Michael in *him*, not he serving

Michael, but Michael serving him, because the Christ-force is in him' (Ita Wegman, Ed. P. Selg, *Erinnerung an Rudolf Steiner*. Op. cit.; italics Ita Wegman).

190. In earlier editions the word 'wants' was still set in italics by Marie Steiner, because she could remember how forcefully Rudolf Steiner had pronounced it.
191. In my view, there is no doubt that had he not become ill at the end of September 1924, Rudolf Steiner would have resumed in October the recapitulation lessons in the context of the First Class of the School of Spiritual Science.
192. There is no mention of this in Bruno Krüger's memoirs. (See B. Krüger, *Leben und Schicksal. Vom Weg eines Wahrheitssuchers*. Freiburg 1993.)
193. When one thinks that Rudolf Steiner—as he himself always emphasized—formed the Executive Council in conjunction with the spiritual world and for this reason considered it an esoteric Council ('Therefore, since this Christmas Conference in Dornach it must be recognized that the establishment of the Dornach Executive Council is itself esoteric', GA 260a, 16 April 1924), it would in my opinion be entirely impossible that he had not communicated to members of the Executive Council something with such immense spiritual consequences for the entire Anthroposophical Movement as a failure of the Christmas Conference. And this view is further supported by the fact that if the Christmas Conference had failed, then the Executive Council would have lost its real esoteric task. Above all, it is not conceivable that Rudolf Steiner had not said anything about the emergence of such an entirely new situation to Marie Steiner, Ita Wegman, Albert Steffen, Günther Wachsmuth or Polzer-Hoditz (see Note 198), who all, even during the time of his illness, visited him frequently and engaged in various conversations, including the topics of the Christmas Conference and the School of Spiritual Science.
194. Thus, there appeared on 3 May 1925 in the *Nachrichtenblatt* the first mutual communication of the Executive Council to the members, which began with the sentence: 'The leadership of the Anthroposophical Society will be conducted further in the same manner designated by Rudolf Steiner in the Christmas Conference.' Also, it is further mentioned in this 'communication' how the admissions into the Society and the School of Spiritual Science would be conducted: exactly in the same way Rudolf Steiner maintained it until his death. (About this see pp. 82–84 of this book.)
195. See S.O. Prokofieff/P. Selg: *The Creative Power of Anthroposophical Christology*. SteinerBooks 2012. Part 4: *The Christmas Conference and the Founding of the New Mysteries*, Appendix.
196. How seriously Rudolf Steiner took the signing of the pink cards is proven alone by the fact that after the Christmas Conference he signed 12,000

membership cards with his own hand. He reported about this as follows: 'Therefore, I have also decided ... to sign every single certificate myself. Work out for yourself what that means with 12,000 members!' (GA 260a, 29 March 1924). He added in another place, 'That is of course a work of many weeks' (GA 260a, 5 September 1924). But as chairman of the Anthroposophical Society he did not want to delegate this work to anyone, not even the other Executive Council members.

197. GA 260, 28 December 1923.

198. When one thinks that the founding of the School of Spiritual Science was possible only out of the new 'esoteric impulse' which entered the entire Anthroposophical Movement and Society at the Christmas Conference, then all of Rudolf Steiner's statements about the full relevance of the Michael School—also during the time of his illness—receive their full significance. For at the same time they give evidence of the further working and living of the Christmas Conference. Thus, for example, on 11 November 1924, Rudolf Steiner discussed extensively with Ludwig Polzer-Hoditz the structure of the three Classes, with the important remark that he wanted to have the First Class conducted by Ita Wegman and the Second Class by Marie Steiner. He wanted to take leadership of the Third Class himself (see GA 260a, *Chronik 1924–1925*). And during his final meeting with Polzer-Hoditz on 3 March 1925, where discussion once again took place on the topic of the Christmas Conference and the School of Spiritual Science, Rudolf Steiner said: 'Whenever and wherever you hold the Class Lessons, take care at all times that during the Lessons you do not feel the need to bring a lively lecture to the reading, rather that you are in an activity, have to achieve an activity that can place us in connection with the Mystery-stream of all times' (T.H. Meyer, *Ludwig Polzer-Hoditz. Ein Europeäer.* Appendix VI, Basel 1994). This connection with the central Mystery-stream of humanity was however only possible as a result of the Christmas Conference, directly through which was created the basis (and the Foundation Stone) for the New Mysteries.—In addition, such close colleagues of Rudolf Steiner's like Marie Steiner and Ita Wegman remained true to the fundamental impulse of the Michael School until the end of their lives. Thus, Marie Steiner felt herself as the co-director of the School until the end. In a letter from 23 October 1947, she wrote to a number of members of the School: 'You ask me as legitimate member of the Executive Council and co-director of the School to confirm this right to free activity in the School and the Society. This I do from the bottom of my heart' (Marie Steiner, *Briefe und Dokumente.* Dornach 1984). Therefore, her intentions in the last year of her life moved her to integrate the Nachlassverein, which she founded, into the School of Spiritual Science. 'The Nachlassverein must continue to exist as part of the School', she wrote on 2 April 1946 (ibid.). For

her part, Ita Wegman remarked in a letter: 'I have heard much about this [Michael] School from Rudolf Steiner, also his and my relationship to it. As the most essential thing that came about through the Christmas Conference, I want to connect myself strongly with this impulse and act out of it' (P. Selg, *Rudolf Steiner and the School for Spiritual Science. The Foundation of the 'First Class'*. SteinerBooks 2012, letter of 22 February 1935 to Marie Röschl). The last Class Lesson held by Ita Wegman took place only three months before her death in 1943.

199. On 8 February 1925, the relationship of the General Anthroposophical Society founded at the Christmas Conference to the 'Goetheanum Building Association', at that time already entered in the trade register, was also legally regulated. Although Rudolf Steiner could not participate in this assembly of the Building Association due to his illness, all decisions by those present were made according to his intentions. That he was also in agreement with this can be seen from the fact that he co-signed the 'Application for the Trade Register' resulting from it, in which all decisions were compiled (see GA 260a, pp. 564–566).

200. 'The ideal condition is above all that one has been a member [of the Society] for at least two years' (GA 260a, 12 August 1924).

201. The applications are printed as facsimiles in the book by S.O. Prokofieff/P. Selg, *The Creative Power of Anthroposophical Christology*. SteinerBooks 2012. Part 4: 'The Christmas Conference and the Founding of the New Mysteries', Appendix.

202. GA 260a, 18 January 1924; 25 January 1924.

203. GA 152, 2 May 1913.

204. 'Why do we concern ourselves with spiritual science? It is as though we were learning the vocabulary of that language through which we approach the Christ.... Let us then try to acquire spiritual science, not as a mere doctrine, but as a language, then wait until we can find the questions which we may venture to put to Christ. He *will* answer; yes, He will answer!' (GA 175, 6 February 1917; italics Rudolf Steiner).

205. See GA 130, 17 September 1911.

206. In the third set of notes for Édouard Schuré in September 1907, Rudolf Steiner wrote that the 'real *meaning of the Earth* consists in the knowledge and realization of the intentions of the *living Christ*. The most deep-seated goal of Rosicrucianism is to unveil this in the form of full wisdom, beauty and deed' (GA 262, p. 26; italics Rudolf Steiner). Anthroposophy is the present continuation of Rosicrucianism. Also, in many other places Rudolf Steiner connects the goal of Earth-development with the Christ being and His deed on Golgotha. (See, for example, GA 97, Questions and Answers on the lecture of 3 February 1907; GA 132, 14 November 1911; GA 152, 2 May 1913.)

207. Because all of anthroposophy, as modern revelation of the continued activity of the Christ impulse, is inseparably connected with this meaning and future of the Earth, Rudolf Steiner could speak these weighty words about it: 'Either the Earth has a future or it hasn't. The Earth's future is inseparable from anthroposophy. If anthroposophy has no future, mankind as a whole has no future either. *The tendency is alone sufficient*' (GA 217a, 8 February 1923). Unfortunately, this tendency has been fading more and more even in the Goetheanum. (See also the epigraph to the Preface.)

208. Regarding the goal of humanity on Earth, which consists in the development of the individual human 'I', see GA 13 and GA 130, 9 January 1912.

209. 'Man is spirit. And his world is that of the spirits' (GA 26, article: 'The Way of Michael and What Preceded It'; italics Rudolf Steiner).

210. Ita Wegman wrote in one of her notebooks in this regard: 'The picture we have of Rudolf Steiner hasn't faded in the course of the years. To the contrary, it is livelier and fresher. This is proof that Rudolf Steiner is connected with us despite his leaving, and one could see the truth in the phrase: Although spiritually removed, yet still very near. One feels this closeness' (P. Selg, *Rudolf Steiner as a Spiritual Teacher. From Recollections of Those Who Knew Him.* SteinerBooks 2010).—In the written notes of her lecture about Rudolf Steiner in London on 27 February 1931, she clearly expressed the two main conditions necessary for such an inner connection with Rudolf Steiner. The first condition is the 'understanding for the ideas of the Christmas Conference'. For only the understanding of this central deed of Rudolf Steiner's could—so she writes—hold him still for a longer period of time on Earth. 'As that does not appear to be the case, he has left us.' But even after his death this question of *understanding* remains relevant. Ita Wegman writes about this: 'In many people there lives the burning question: "Is Rudolf Steiner still connected with us after his death?"' Her answer is: 'When we didn't understand him during his life, is it possible to understand him now?' When this understanding is forthcoming, then Rudolf Steiner can remain connected even today with the people 'who stand by him'. This can happen only by additionally fulfilling the second condition: 'When such feelings that express *devotion and pure love* rise up to him, a renewed connection with him occurs out of freedom; then he will remain with us and continue to be our teacher beyond life and death' (J.E. Zeylmans van Emmichoven, *Who Was Ita Wegman. A Documentation, Vol. I—1876 until 1925*. Mercury Press 1995). Thus, this connection with Rudolf Steiner is possible at all times for members of the Anthroposophical Society, when, selflessly and in freedom, they fulfil these two conditions.

211. In the third Mystery Drama, *The Guardian of the Threshold* (GA 14), Benedictus says:

>I must accompany everyone who receives
>The spirit light from me in Earth-being,
>Whether he devoted himself knowingly
>Or only unconsciously to me as spiritual pupil,
>And must accompany him further on the path
>That he treaded through me in spirit.
>(6th Act)

212. In this sense, Ehrenfried Pfeiffer wrote in his letter of 29 February 1948, to Marie Steiner: 'Only when we hold this sacrifice or Mystery-deed of Rudolf Steiner's [at the Christmas Conference] continually before us in our souls can Rudolf Steiner work through us and the [Anthroposophical] Society, and use it as a physical instrument' (S.O. Prokofieff/ P. Selg, *The Creative Power of Anthroposophical Christology*. SteinerBooks 2012. Part 4: 'The Christmas Conference and the Founding of the New Mysteries', Section II by S.O. Prokofieff, 'The Being of the Christmas Conference and Its Sources of Inspiration'). Marie Steiner answered this letter from Ehrenfried Pfeiffer on 11 March 1948 (in the year of her death): 'You have described Rudolf Steiner's Mystery-deed beautifully' (ibid.). Then Ehrenfried Pfeiffer further developed his conviction in this regard in his open letter of 5 March 1948, to the Executive Council and the Annual General Meeting of the members at Easter 1948: 'If this Society, comprised of all those who want to follow Rudolf Steiner, intends in all reality to continue existing on Earth—then Rudolf Steiner could even today work out of the spiritual world through the [Anthroposophical] Society as leader and chairman' (ibid.).

213. During the lecture, the enlarged photo was displayed on an easel on the stage of the Great Hall, next to the lectern.

214. 'But Michael's impulses are strong, are powerful, and they work from the spirit into the whole of man's being; they work into the spirit, from there into the soul, and from there into the bodily nature of man' (GA 237, 3 August 1924).

215. 'For if we sum up all that I have said of Michaelism (if I may now so call it) then we shall find: The Michaelites are indeed taken hold of in their souls by a power that is seeking to work from the spiritual into the full human being, even down into the physical' (GA 237, 4 August 1924).

216. 'For the first time, the spiritual is preparing to become a race-creating force. [That is, the spirit will enter all the way into the physical, transforming it and revealing itself therein.] The time will come when one will no longer be able to say: This man looks as if he belonged to this or that country—he is a Turk, or Arab, an Englishman, a Russian or a German—but one will have to say what will amount to this: "In a former life on Earth this man felt impelled to turn towards the Spirit in the sense of Michael." Thus, that

which is influenced by Michael will appear as an immediate, physically creative, physically formative power' (GA 237, 3 August 1924).

217. About this see in W. Beck, *Rudolf Steiner—die letzen drie Jahre*. Dornach 1985.
218. 'For it is this which so rightly brings us closer to the great, important mission of anthroposophy: that anthroposophy will bridge the abyss between the living and the dead' (GA 141, 4 March 1913).
219. See GA 182, 30 April 1918.—In summer 1918, during his visit to Prague, Rudolf Steiner said to the Czech anthroposophist Julie Klima: 'A time will come when the dead will rule the nations' (J. Klima, *Erinnerungen an Rudolf Steiner*. Prague 1928; published in the Appendix in Ludwig Polzer-Hoditz, *Erinnerungen an Rudolf Steiner*. Dornach 1985).
220. Rudolf Steiner said that the sixth cultural epoch must be prepared for by anthroposophical work today in GA 159, 15 June 1915, as well as in the lecture of 3 February 1913, 'The Being Anthroposophy', published in the compilation *Schicksalszeichen auf dem Entwicklungsweg der Anthroposophischen Gesellschaft*. Dornach 1943.
221. In the 'epilogue' to his book of poetry *We Have Found a Path*, Christian Morgenstern summarized the importance of his life's acquaintance with Rudolf Steiner as follows:

> You pure spirit,
> From your strong hands
> I renew my sense of life.

(Christian Morgenstern, *Werke und Briefe, Vol. II*, 'Lyrics 1906 to 1914'. Stuttgart 1992. In English: *We Have Found a Path*, Mercury Press / *We Found a Path*, Pegasus Publishing.)
222. Quoted from Christian Morgenstern, *We Have Found a Path*, Mercury Press / *We Found a Path*, Pegasus Publishing.
223. GA 159, 31 October 1914.
224. From a letter to Madeleine van Deventer in 1942. (P. Selg, *Die letzen drie Jahre. Ita Wegman in Ascona. 1940 to 1943*. Chapter 4, Dornach 2004.)
225. However, with the decisive difference that for this exemplary friendship of two poets to take place, Schiller had to overcome his envy, his resentment and his inferiority-complex towards Goethe through pure love and complete respect (devotion) for the merits of the other. Rudolf Steiner said in this regard: 'He [Schiller] had difficulty making up his mind to appreciate Goethe. Schiller proceeded from envy and from inner aversion towards Goethe' (GA 191, 14 November 1919). As Schiller nevertheless succeeded in so transforming and cleansing his relationship to Goethe, it became for him a kind of 'religion', whose foundation was the pure love for his friend. About this he wrote to Goethe in the following words: 'The beautiful relationship that exists between us, I turn it into a kind of religion, to make

your affair mine, all that is reality in me; to develop it into the purest mirror of the spirit who lives in this body, and so in a higher sense of the word to deserve to be called your friend. By this opportunity, how actively have I experienced that excellence is a power, that it can only work as a power in selfish souls when with respect to excellence there is no freedom other than love' (H. Koopmann, *Schillers Leben in Briefen*. letter from 2 July 1796, Weimar 2000). These words reveal, like hardly any others, the greatness of Schiller's soul. Only through this self-overcoming out of the force of the 'I' did Schiller become Goethe's co-equal. (See S.O. Prokofieff, *Friedrich Schiller und die Zukunft der Freiheit. Zugleich einige Aspekte seiner okkulten Biographie*. Dornach 2007. Chapter 1, 'Der geistige Auftrag Schillers zwischen Goethe und Novalis'.)—At the same time, Goethe did not make it easy for Schiller to approach him. His aversion to Schiller's stormy early work was so great that he avoided the meeting with Schiller for more than six years (from 1788 to 1794), whereby Schiller, who had long before overcome himself inwardly, suffered greatly. In retrospect, Schiller regretted that due to Goethe's dismissive treatment their friendship had begun so late. (Regarding this see P. Selg, *Friedrich Schiller. Die Geistigkeit des Willens*. Dornach 2010. Chapter II, 'Goethe und Schiller'.)

226. 'He [the spiritual pupil] can now discern the great differences among human beings with regard to their level of development. He becomes aware that there are men of higher rank than his own who have already reached the stages which still lie ahead of him . . . He owes this knowledge to his own first glimpse into this higher world. The persons called the "great Initiates of humanity" will now begin to be realities for him' (GA 10, Chapter: 'Some Effects of Initiation').

227. This means not only highly developed human individuals (the Masters), but also Hierarchical beings such as Angels, Archangels and so forth.

228. F. Rittelmeyer, *Rudolf Steiner Enters My Life*, reprint in preparation by Floris Books, 2013.—In his early anthroposophical correspondence, Rudolf Steiner continually writes with deepest respect and reverence for the great initiates and pure spiritual beings that act as the inspiring forces behind the Anthroposophical Movement. Thus, for example, in the letter of 12 August 1904: 'In such [esoteric] matters I am only the instrument of higher beings, whom I revere in *humility*' (GA 264; italics Rudolf Steiner). This motif appears frequently in esoteric lessons. (See also GA 264, 2 January 1905.)

229. GA 155, 14 July 1914.

230. Lecture from 28 March 1915 in Dornach. Quoted from the compilation: Rudolf Steiner, *Christian Morgenstern. Der Sieg des Lebens über den Tod*. Dornach 1935.

231. See the previous Note.—Further, Christian Morgenstern became the

spiritual leader of many recently dead souls who were in the spiritual world. Rudolf Steiner reported about this as follows: 'Thus, Christian Morgenstern appears to me today after his death as the spiritual leader of many people who, in the recent past of mankind's spiritual development, have risen into the spiritual worlds and with this experience a tremendous challenge . . .' (ibid., lecture of 7 October 1914).

232. Christian Morgenstern: *Gesammelte Werke in einem Band*. Munich 1974.

233. Christian Morgenstern, *We Have Found a Path*, Mercury Press / *We Found a Path*, Pegasus Publishing.

234. In a close circle of her friends, Ita Wegman said that Rudolf Steiner mentioned to her 'that Christian Rosenkreuz and his hosts moved into the "Schreinerei" for the Christmas Foundation Stone-laying' (M. and E. Kirchner-Bockholt, *Rudolf Steiner's Mission and Ita Wegman*, Chapter: 'Rudolf Steiner's Mission', private printing by the Anthroposophical Society in Great Britain, 1974).

235. GA 260, 1 January 1924, *Aus dem Mitgliederkreise*. Louis M.J. Werbeck (1879–1928) was a courageous and uncompromising fighter of all opponents of Rudolf Steiner and anthroposophy. In 1924 he published his two-volume authoritative work about the opponents under the summarizing motto, *Eine Gegnerschaft als Kultur-Verfallserscheinung* Vol. I, *Die christlichen Gegner Rudolf Steiners und der Anthroposophie durch sie selbst widerlegt*, and Vol. II, *Die wissenschaftlichen Gegner Rudolf Steiners und der Anthroposophie durch sie selbst widerlegt*, Stuttgart 1924. If a person reads these two volumes, he will be surprised that today most opponents again come forward with the same pseudo-scientific arguments, thought-clichés, lies and slander. However, gratitude towards Rudolf Steiner and the courage to defend him in public—both of which Louis Werbeck possessed—have visibly decreased since then in the Anthroposophical Society and above all within many of its leading committees.

236. Regarding this see S.O. Prokofieff, *May Human Beings Hear It! The Mystery of the Christmas Conference*. Temple Lodge 2004.

237. This article first appeared in *Das Goetheanum*, issue 27: 7 July 2012. For Peter Selg's publication, see Part I of this book.

238. *Twelve Moods*: from the 'Capricorn Verse', GA 40; Published as a booklet by Mercury Press.

239. The theme of the 'Constitution' gave rise to a total of over 2,000 pages of text in Central Europe alone.

240. What is meant is the culmination of *anthroposophy* (not its daughter movements, as some anthroposophists mistakenly believe even still today) at the end of the last century, about which Rudolf Steiner had spoken with great earnestness and contemplation in many of the Karma lectures. (See for example GA 237: 28 July 1924 and 8 August 1924; GA 240 / *Karmic*

Relationships Vols. VI and VIII: 18 July 1924 [from Vol. VI]; 14 August 1924 and 27 August 1924 [from Vol. VIII].)

241. See GA 258, 16 June 1923; and GA 259, 17 June 1923 (the latter is included in the English volume *The Anthroposophic Movement / GA 258*).

242. See GA 260a, 18 January 1924 (in English: *The Constitution of the School of Spiritual Science*); and 6 February 1924 (not translated).

243. Regarding this see also S.O. Prokofieff, *Relating to Rudolf Steiner. The Mystery of the Laying of the Foundation Stone.* Temple Lodge 2008.

244. P. Selg, lecture of 30 March 2012. See Part I of this book, 'The Challenges of the Present and Future'.

245. In a lecture of 16 May 1920 (GA 201), Rudolf Steiner also named Parzival as a representative of humanity.—On the relation of Rudolf Steiner to the modern Parzival-task, see further in S.O. Prokofieff, *Rudolf Steiner and the Founding of the New Mysteries.* Temple Lodge 1994. Chapter 7, 'The Michael-Age and the New Grail Event'.

246. GA 259, p. 530, italics Rudolf Steiner; likewise for the next citation.—In other places, Rudolf Steiner expressed himself still more radically in relation to the opponents who lie publicly, pointing out that when someone publishes falsehoods about anthroposophy it is the duty of anthroposophists to designate this publicly as lies. If one does not do this, for whatever well-meant reasons, then one shows that he *loves the lies* and becomes, whether he wants to or not, a co-conspirator of the lies. When one thinks that from the occult point of view the lie is a murder on the astral plane (see GA 94, 2 June 1906), then he can measure the importance of the further statement: 'Whoever has something against pronouncing [such lies publicly], he loves the lies. And who says we polemicize too much when we characterize the truth correctly, he has no sense for the truth and loves the lies. And of those who love lies, that shall not be our business within the Anthroposophical Society, but we must love the truth. The complete importance of these words must be felt: To love the truth—and not the lies for the sake of convention, for the sake of pleasant society life. For indulging lies is no different than loving the lies. The world will come to truth in the near future not through being frivolously indifferent towards falsity, but alone through the free and fresh commitment to truth' (GA 197, 22 November 1920).

247. See GA 240, 20 July, 1924 (in English: *Karmic Relationships* Vol. VI).

248. See S.O. Prokofieff: 'Ein Buch und seine Hintergründe' [A Book and Its Background], and 'Blick auf der Gegnerschaft' [A Glimpse of the Opposition], two essays in '*Nachrichtenblatt*' [the *Das Goetheanum* members' newsletter/insert which has since been discontinued], No. 45 and No. 46 / 2007.

249. Quoted from P. Selg, lecture of 30 March 2012. See Part I of this book, 'The Challenges of the Present and Future'.

250. GA 260a, 25 January 1924 (not translated).
251. Regarding this see the testimonies of the two closest colleagues and students of Rudolf Steiner, Marie Steiner and Ita Wegman, in S.O. Prokofieff / P. Selg, *The Creative Power of Anthroposophical Christology*. SteinerBooks 2012. Part 4, 'The Christmas Conference and the Founding of the New Mysteries', Section II by S.O. Prokofieff: 'The Nature of the Christmas Conference and Its Sources of Inspiration'.

Bibliography

English titles of works by Rudolf Steiner are given only in cases where a similar (though not always identical) volume to the original German edition from the collected works—the Gesamtausgabe (abbreviated as 'GA')—has been published in English translation. In many cases, lectures are available in typescript or in print as single lectures or compilations from the collected works. For information on these contact Rudolf Steiner House Library, 35 Park Road, London NW1 6XT, or similar anthroposophically-based libraries around the world.

RSP = Rudolf Steiner Press
AP = Anthroposophic Press/SteinerBooks
MP = Mercury Press

GA 9	*Theosophy* (RSP and AP)
GA 10	*Knowledge of the Higher Worlds: How is it Achieved?* (RSP; AP: *How to Know Higher Worlds*)
GA 13	*Occult Science: An Outline* (RSP; AP: *An Outline of Esoteric Science*)
GA 14	*Four Mystery Dramas* (AP)
GA 26	*Anthroposophical Leading Thoughts* (RSP)
GA 28	*An Autobiography / The Course of My Life* (AP)
GA 34	*Lucifer-Gnosis. Grundlegende Aufsätze zur Anthroposophie und Berichte aus den Zeitschriften 'Luzifer' und 'Lucifer-Gnosis' 1903–1908*
GA 40	*Wahrspruchworte* (extracts appear in *Verses and Meditations*, RSP; *Twelve Moods*, MP)
GA 51	*Über Philosophie, Geschichte und Literatur*
GA 59	*Metamorphosen des Seelenlebens*
GA 93	*The Temple Legend and the Golden Legend* (RSP)
GA 94	*An Esoteric Cosmology* (AP)
GA 96	*Original Impulses for the Science of the Spirit* (Completion Press)
GA 97	*The Christian Mystery* (Completion Press)
GA 113	*The East in the Light of the West* (RSP and AP)
GA 114	*The Gospel of St Luke* (RSP and AP)
GA 130	*Esoteric Christianity and the Mission of Christian Rosenkreutz* (RSP)
GA 131	*From Jesus to Christ* (RSP)
GA 132	*The Inner Realities of Evolution* (RSP)
GA 136	*The Spiritual Beings in the Heavenly Bodies and in the Kingdoms of Nature* (AP)
GA 141	*Life Between Death and Rebirth* (RSP)
GA 148	*The Fifth Gospel* (RSP)
GA 152	*Approaching the Mystery of Golgotha* (AP)

GA 155	*Christ and the Human Soul* (RSP)
GA 159	*Das Geheimnis des Todes*
GA 170	*The Riddle of Humanity* (RSP)
GA 175	*Building Stones to the Understanding of the Mystery of Golgotha* (RSP)
GA 182	*Death as a Metamorphosis of Life* (AP)
GA 191	*Soziales Verständnis aus Zukunftsimpulse und Auferstehungsgedanke*
GA 193	*Der innere Aspekt des sozialen Rätsels. Luziferische Vergangenheit und ahrimanische Zukunft*
	Fragments in English: *The Esoteric Aspect of the Social Question* (RSP)
GA 197	*Polarities in the Evolution of Mankind* (RSP/AP)
GA 201	*Mystery of the Universe. The Human Being, Image of Creation* [Formerly *Man, Hieroglyph of the Universe*] (RSP)
GA 202	*The Bridge Between Universal Spirituality and the Physical Constitution of Man* (AP); *The Search for the New Isis* (MP)
GA 217	*Becoming the Archangel Michael's Companions* (AP)
GA 217a	*Youth and the Etheric Heart* (AP)
GA 221	*Earthly Knowledge and Heavenly Wisdom* (AP)
GA 223	*Anthroposophy and the Human Gemüt* (AP)
GA 231	*Supersensible Man* (Garber Communications), *At Home in the Universe* (RSP)
GA 232	*Mystery Knowledge and Mystery Centres* (RSP)
GA 233a	*Mysterienstätten des Mittelalters. Rosenkreuzertum und modernes Einweihungsprinzip. Das Osterfest als ein Stück Mysteriengeschichte der Menschheit*
	Fragments in English: *Rosicrucianism and Modern Initiation* (RSP) and *The Easter Festival* (RSP)
GA 237	*Karmic Relationships, Vol. III* (RSP)
GA 240	*Karmic Relationships, Vol. VI* (RSP) and *Karmic Relationships, Vol. VIII* (RSP)
GA 255b	*Die Anthroposophie und ihre Gegner 1919–1921*
GA 257	*Awakening to Community* (AP)
GA 258	*The Anthroposophic Movement* (RSP)
GA 259	*Das Schicksalsjahr 1923 in der Geschichte der Anthroposophischen Gesellschaft. Vom Goetheanumbrand zur Weihnachtstagung (1923)* [The Year of Destiny 1923 in the History of the Anthroposophical Society: From the Burning of the Goetheanum to the Christmas Conference]
GA 260	*The Christmas Conference for the Foundation of the General Anthroposophical Society 1923/1924* (AP)
GA 260a	*Die Konstitution der Allgemeinen Anthroposophischen Gesellschaft und der Freien Hochschule für Geisteswissenschaft. Der Wiederaufbau des Goetheanum (1924–1925)*

	Fragments in English: *The Life, Nature and Cultivation of Anthroposophy* and *The Constitution of the School of Spiritual Science* (both published by the Anthroposophical Society in Great Britain, and reprinted as *The Foundation Stone*, RSP)
GA 262	*Correspondence and Documents 1901–1925. Rudolf Steiner and Marie Steiner von Sivers* (RSP)
GA 263a	*Rudolf Steiner / Edith Maryon: Briefwechsel. Briefe—Sprüche—Skizzen, 1912–1924*
GA 264	*From the History and Contents of the First Section of the Esoteric School 1904–1914: Letters, Documents, and Lectures* (AP)
GA 270a, c	*Esoterische Unterweisungen für die erste Klasse der Freien Hochschule für Geisteswissenschaft am Goetheanum 1924*
GA 286	*Architecture as a Synthesis of the Arts* (RSP)
GA 300c	*Faculty Meetings with Rudolf Steiner* (AP)
GA 303	*Soul Economy and Waldorf Education* (AP / RSP)
GA 307	*Modern Art of Education* (RSP)
GA 308	*Essentials of Education* (AP)
GA 316	*Course for Young Doctors* (MP)
GA 318	*Broken Vessels. The Spiritual Structure of Human Frailty* [formerly *Pastoral Medicine*] (AP)
GA 330	*Neuegestaltung des sozialen Organismus*
	Fragments in English: *The Renewal of the Social Organism* (AP 1996)
GA 346	*The Book of Revelation and the Work of the Priest* (RSP)

Works by Rudolf Steiner are available via Rudolf Steiner Press, UK (www.rudolfsteinerpress.com) or SteinerBooks, USA (www.steinerbooks.org).